# KINGDOM AGENDA

BIBLE STUDY

## TONY EVANS

LIVING LIFE GOD'S WAY

LifeWay Press®
Nashville, Tennessee

Published by LifeWay Press®
© 2013 Tony Evans

ISBN 978-1-4158-7786-9
Item 005558792

Dewey decimal classification: 248.84
Subject headings: CHRISTIAN LIFE \ SPIRITUAL LIFE \ KINGDOM OF GOD

To order additional copies of this resource, write to LifeWay Church Resources Customer Service; One
LifeWay Plaza; Nashville, TN 37234-0113; fax 615.251.5933; phone toll free 800.458.2772; order online at
*www.lifeway.com;* email *orderentry@lifeway.com;* or visit the LifeWay Christian Store serving you.

*Printed in the United States of America*

Adult Ministry Publishing
LifeWay Church Resources
One LifeWay Plaza
Nashville, TN 37234-0152

# CONTENTS

THE AUTHOR
4

INTRODUCTION
5

WEEK 1
*The Foundations of God's Kingdom Agenda*
7

WEEK 2
*One Life Under God*
35

WEEK 3
*One Family Under God*
63

WEEK 4
*One Church Under God*
91

WEEK 5
*One Nation Under God*
119

WEEK 6
*Living God's Kingdom Agenda*
147

# THE AUTHOR * DR. TONY EVANS

Dr. Tony Evans is one of America's most respected leaders in evangelical circles. He is a pastor, a best-selling author, and a frequent speaker at Bible conferences and seminars throughout the nation.

Dr. Evans has served as the senior pastor of Oak Cliff Bible Fellowship for more than 35 years, witnessing its growth from 10 people in 1976 to more than 9,000 congregants with more than one hundred ministries.

Dr. Evans also serves as the president of The Urban Alternative, a national ministry that seeks to bring about spiritual renewal in America through the church. His daily radio broadcast, "The Alternative with Dr. Tony Evans," can be heard on 850 radio outlets throughout the United States and in more than 115 countries.

Dr. Evans has authored more than 50 books, including *Oneness Embraced, The Kingdom Agenda, Marriage Matters, Kingdom Man, Victory in Spiritual Warfare,* and *God's Unlikely Path to Success.* Dr. Evans, a former chaplain for the NFL Dallas Cowboys, is currently the chaplain for the NBA's Dallas Mavericks, a team he has served for more than 30 years.

Through his local church and national ministry, Dr. Evans has set in motion a kingdom-agenda philosophy of ministry that teaches God's comprehensive rule over every area of life, as demonstrated through the individual, family, church, and society.

Dr. Evans is married to Lois, his wife and ministry partner of more than 40 years. They are the proud parents of four— Chrystal, Priscilla, Anthony Jr., and Jonathan.

# INTRODUCTION

I've written a number of books and Bible studies throughout my years in ministry, but I consider this study, *Kingdom Agenda,* to be my magnum opus. This study uniquely expresses my comprehensive worldview, philosophy of life, and philosophy of ministry. More importantly, I consider this study important for every believer because it fundamentally addresses the kingdom of God and His agenda for us as members of that kingdom.

When I use the term *kingdom agenda,* I'm referring to God's blueprint for the way He wants us to live as His followers here on earth. This is vital information, and it needs to remain at the forefront of our thinking in order for that blueprint to fully penetrate our choices and decisions. When that happens, we're in a position to fully realize God's covenant authority and blessings.

Sadly, this message of God's kingdom agenda is sorely lacking today, even in the church. That's not to say that we don't speak about God's kingdom in the church; we do. But too much of what we say is esoteric, theological code words that are unrelated to the realities of life in the here and now.

The absence of a comprehensive agenda for life has led to deterioration of cosmic proportions. Few followers of Christ have developed a true kingdom worldview, and the result has been chaos and confusion in all areas of life. We live segmented, compartmentalized lives as individuals because we lack an overarching blueprint to give us direction. Families disintegrate because they exist for their own fulfillment. Churches have a limited impact on society because they fail to understand that the goal of the church is not the church itself but the kingdom. Society at large has nowhere to turn for solid solutions to the perplexing challenges that confront us today, including a myriad of social ills.

It's time for Christians to recognize our place as citizens of God's kingdom. We need a comprehensive worldview based on the way our Creator intended every area of life to be lived. We need an agenda big enough to include both individuals and societal structures, clear enough to be understood and appropriated by the average person on the street, and flexible enough to allow for considerable differences among peoples and societies.

In other words, we need God's kingdom agenda.

# HERE'S HOW IT WORKS

This member book includes content for both individual and group study. The best way to learn God's kingdom ways and priorities is to engage in individual, daily devotions and to participate in a Bible-study group that includes video teaching and discussion.

Each week's study begins with a suggested process for a group experience. Each group session should follow this general outline.

**START.** Begin each session with a brief time of discussion that helps you and your group get to know one another better and discuss what the Lord has taught you during the previous week.

**WATCH.** Your group will watch a 30-minute teaching segment on DVD while completing the viewer guide provided in each group experience.

**RESPOND.** Use the suggested questions to discuss the truths presented on the DVD. Then close each group experience with prayer. Each session wraps up with a key verse of Scripture to memorize and a specific challenge to tackle the next week.

The teaching segment and group discussion will provide a foundation for your individual study throughout the week. Each day you'll read a devotion that fleshes out the Scriptures and ideas first presented in the group experience. You'll also complete personal learning activities that will help you move toward God's kingdom agenda. If you complete each week's personal study, you'll arrive at your next group session ready to begin another discussion based on the individual work you've done.

Throughout these six sessions you'll find a new perspective on what it means to be a citizen of God's kingdom. As you study biblical truths about your identity and role in the kingdom, you'll learn to exercise the rights, authority, and responsibilities God has granted you as His representative on earth whom He's commissioned to make an eternal difference in your family, your church, your community, and your world.

If you want to explore the kingdom agenda further after completing this study, read Tony Evans's book *The Kingdom Agenda: Life Under God* (Moody Publishers).

Week 1

# THE FOUNDATIONS OF GOD'S KINGDOM AGENDA

# START

**Welcome to this small-group discussion of Kingdom Agenda.**

To facilitate introductions and to focus on the theme of *Kingdom Agenda*, spend a few moments talking as a group about the process of building a house from scratch. Use the following questions to guide your conversation.

- What experiences have you had with building or remodeling projects?

- In your opinion or based on your experience, what are the most difficult aspects of building a new house from scratch? Why?

- Which features or additional elements would turn a good house into your ideal house?

How would you define or summarize *kingdom of God* in your own words?

Spend a few minutes as a group comparing and contrasting the values of God's kingdom with the values of our modern culture. (Consider creating a Venn diagram if a whiteboard or a large sheet of paper is available.)

To prepare for the DVD segment, read aloud the following verses.

> Pilate entered again into the Praetorium, and summoned Jesus and said to Him, "Are You the King of the Jews?" Jesus answered, "Are you saying this on your own initiative, or did others tell you about Me?" Pilate answered, "I am not a Jew, am I? Your own nation and the chief priests delivered You to me; what have You done?" Jesus answered, "My kingdom is not of this world. If My kingdom were of this world, then My servants would be fighting so that I would not be handed over to the Jews; but as it is, My kingdom is not of this realm." Therefore Pilate said to Him, "So You are a king?" Jesus answered, "You say correctly that I am a king. For this I have been born, and for this I have come into the world, to testify to the truth. Everyone who is of the truth hears My voice."
>
> JOHN 18:33-37

## WATCH

***Complete the viewer guide below as you watch DVD session 1.***

The kingdom agenda is the visible demonstration of the comprehensive _____ of _____ over every area of life.

God created man to demonstrate His greater _____ and to advance His _____ in history.

God has a kingdom but only if He is _____.

Worldliness is _____ against kingdomness.

God wants us in the world, but He doesn't want the world in _____.

The world is the system headed by Satan that wants to leave _____ out.

The reason God's kingdom is not fixing what's wrong in our world is that the folks who want God to fix it are simultaneously _____.

If you belong to Jesus Christ, this world is not your _____.

The truth is the absolute _____ by which reality is measured.

God does not leave His kingdom to satisfy our _____ in this world. He invites us from this world into His kingdom.

If you want your life and our world on target, then God must be recognized as the comprehensive _____ of this kingdom.

Unless God is free to call the shots, the _____ we need in our lives will not happen.

# RESPOND

*Use the following questions to discuss the DVD segment with your group.*

What did you appreciate most in Dr. Evans's teaching? Why?

Think over your definition or summary of *kingdom of God* from earlier in the group session. What would you change after hearing Dr. Evans speak?

Which rules or guidelines are most important in your home?

Which rules or guidelines seem most important in God's kingdom?

Respond to Dr. Evans's statement: "The reason God's kingdom is not fixing what's wrong in our world is that the folks who want God to fix it are simultaneously worldly."

What ideas or images come to mind when you hear the word *truth?* Why?

During what periods of life have you felt most connected to and aligned with God's kingdom agenda?

**Application.** As you move through your everday routines this week, be aware of the times when your status as a member of God's kingdom causes tension or dissonance with your status as a participant in today's culture. Consider keeping a journal or taking notes when these clashes occur.

**This week's Scripture memory.**

> *No one can serve two masters; for either he will hate the one and love the other,*
> *or he will be devoted to one and despise the other. You cannot serve God and wealth.*
> MATTHEW 6:24

**Assignment.** Read week 1 and complete the activities before the next group experience.

## OUR TRUE KINGDOM

Do you know what it means to be part of a kingdom? As people living in a constitutional republic like the United States of America, we sometimes have trouble wrapping our minds around the concept of a kingdom, not to mention the consequences of living under the influence and authority of a king.

We have a president in America, of course, but that office is part of our larger governing body. In addition to the executive branch of government, we have legislative and judicial branches. This system of checks and balances was designed to ensure that one person or one group of people doesn't gain too much power and control.

That's not the case in a true kingdom, and that hasn't been the case with the majority of the kingdoms and cultures that have come and gone throughout history. In a true kingdom, all facets of life operate under the direct rule and authority of a king or a queen. The monarch is in charge. The monarch makes decisions and creates laws that steer the course and fortune of the entire nation—for better or for worse.

Therefore, the boundaries of a kingdom extend as far as the influence and control of the king. Wherever a king's direct authority is acknowledged and obeyed, that place is part of the king's realm—part of his kingdom.

It's important for us as Christians to understand these principles because the Bible tells us again and again that we're part of the kingdom of God. We're subjects in God's kingdom, which means we're under the direct authority and rule of God as our King—or we're supposed to be. Too often, however, we drift into rebellion and actively or passively seek to dethrone the One we're supposed to serve.

This week we'll explore foundational biblical components of what it means to live as a subject in God's kingdom and to live under the authority of His kingdom agenda.

# UNDERSTAND THE PROBLEM

I don't know about you, but I hate getting sick. I hate that feeling when my nose starts running, my eyes start watering, and my throat gets scratchy. I hate it when my stomach churns. I hate it when my head aches. I hate it when my mind gets fuzzy.

In other words, I hate the physical symptoms that are almost always connected with illness. Can you relate?

One reason I hate getting sick is that I know the physical symptoms I'm experiencing are evidence of a deep dysfunction in my body. Being sick means something is wrong inside me: a virus or bacterium has penetrated the defenses of my immune system, in turn causing adverse physical reactions in my body. These reactions can range from mildly annoying to life-threatening.

How do you typically react when you get sick?

Which symptoms of common illnesses do you dislike most? Why?

People often ask, What's wrong with the world today? They see people seeking self-help books and counseling because of anxiety, depression, drug abuse, addiction, and a multitude of personal problems. They see the rapid deterioration of the American family. They see the spiritual decline of our nation and the marginalization of the church, though the world desperately needs God's help. They see modern cities and suburbs wracked by crime, violence, racism, and greed.

There's something wrong with the world today, but the deterioration of our society isn't the core problem. Rather, just as physical disease manifests itself in physical symptoms, the dysfunction evident in us as individuals, as families, as a church, and as a nation is merely the symptom of a deeper problem.

In short, our society is suffering from a spiritual sickness. We're in the throes of a spiritual malaise that's been building for decades, and it's killing us.

Of course, sin is the ultimate source of our spiritual sickness. It's the virus that's infected and corrupted all human experience since Adam and Eve took their first bites of the forbidden fruit in rebellion against God.

But I believe a particular manifestation of our sin problem is responsible for the larger spiritual sickness currently attacking modern society. This isn't a new manifestation but one that can be traced all the way back to the struggles and symptoms experienced by the nation of Israel in the Old Testament.

## THE DIAGNOSIS

The following verses from 2 Chronicles 15 capture the essential elements of humanity's current situation:

> *For many days Israel was without the true God and without a teaching priest and without law. In those times there was no peace to him who went out or to him who came in, for many disturbances afflicted all the inhabitants of the lands. Nation was crushed by nation, and city by city, for God troubled them with every kind of distress.*
> 2 CHRONICLES 15:3,5-6

What's your initial reaction to these verses? Why?

How do you see the cultural symptoms described in these verses reflected in our society today?

These verses paint a picture of great spiritual and social chaos—the breakdown of a society. So what was wrong? Three crucial elements were missing in Israelite society, and I believe they're missing today in our nation as well.

## 1. THE ISRAELITES WERE WITHOUT THE TRUE GOD. The

author of these verses wasn't saying God had abandoned His people, nor was he saying the Israelites had become atheists or no longer believed in God. The sacrificial fires were still burning at the temple, and participation in the religious practices was still high.

Rather, Israel had lost an accurate view of God. The Israelites wanted a convenient God—one they could control. They wanted a figurehead who displayed the trappings of authority but carried no real power. Essentially, the Israelites were interested in establishing a kingdom without a King. They didn't want the true God to interfere with their national life, reminding them that He had an agenda greater than their personal interests and desires.

In other words, the people of Israel had forgotten (or had willfully chosen to ignore) that God is the all-powerful, unstoppable Creator of the universe.

> Read the following passages of Scripture and record what they teach about God's true position in relation to humanity.
>
> Exodus 19:18-24
>
> Job 40:1-14
>
> Romans 11:33-36

We've also lost an accurate view of God in today's society. Oh, we're willing to pay homage to Him every now and then in the right circumstances—offering a prayer before public meetings or setting up a nativity scene at Christmas. But mostly we prefer to view Him as a harmless deity with nothing significant to say about the educational, scientific, political, social, familial, and personal issues of our day.

> What evidence have you seen that supports the previous statements?

> When are you tempted to minimize or ignore God's glory and power?

## 2. THE ISRAELITES WERE WITHOUT A TEACHING PRIEST.

Again, the problem wasn't a lack of priests—Israel was filled with priests working in the temple and throughout the nation—but a lack of priests engaged in teaching.

That means the priests of Israel had stopped telling the truth. They'd traded enlightenment for entertainment and allowed genuine worship to degenerate into a social club. As a result, the temple was no longer the epicenter of life and conscience in the culture, calling people to take God seriously. Israel suffered from an absence of spiritual leaders who were serious about the authority of Scripture for all areas of life.

We're also suffering from this absence in the church today. Too many modern pastors preach to please their congregations. Because they're afraid of hearing someone say, "I didn't like that sermon," they abdicate their proper prophetic role in the culture. Politicians need to be popular. Preachers need to tell the truth.

How do you intentionally expose yourself to preaching and teaching that are based on the authority of God's Word?

What steps do you take to apply what you learn?

## 3. THE ISRAELITES WERE WITHOUT LAW. Specifically, they'd
lost an accurate view of and a proper respect for God's law as expressed in His Word. As a result, notice what happened in verse 6:

> *Nation was crushed by nation, and city by city,* ***for God***
> ***troubled them with every kind of distress.***
> 2 CHRONICLES 15:6, emphasis added

You know you're in a bad situation when God is the one troubling you "with every kind of distress"! Yet that's what Israel experienced after they turned their eyes away from the true God, closed their ears to the truth, and turned their backs on God's law.

Once God has been marginalized in a culture, the standards of morality and civility degenerate, and people become their own worst enemies. When the rule of God's law is missing, chaos replaces community as people become more and more enslaved by the very freedoms they seek.

That's what happened in Israel, and that's what's happening in society today. The heart of our problem is that too many individuals, families, churches, and communities want to keep God's law—and by extension God Himself—on the fringes of their lives. They want God to be accessible if there's a critical need or a tragedy, but they don't want to live in submission to His Word or acknowledge it as the source of truth.

How have you seen God's Word marginalized or attacked in today's society?

What steps have you taken to affirm the truth of God's Word and submit to it as your standard of truth?

The spiritual diagnosis for what's wrong with the world today is simple: we've distanced ourselves from God, we've been hesitant to teach the truth about God, and we've refused to submit to God's Word as the law of our lives. And one of the saddest consequences of this spiritual disease is that we've lost our hope.

See, as long as you have God, you have hope. He's the one thing in this whole universe you can bank on with utter certainty—because He created this whole universe. But when God leaves a society, hope goes with Him. When God is marginalized or pushed away by a culture that desires its own rule, hope is marginalized and pushed away with Him. And that's what we're experiencing today.

How have you received hope from your relationship with God?

## THE SOLUTION

What must we do to reverse the spiritual sickness causing this downward spiral in our lives? It's time to return to the King. It's time to place ourselves once again under His rule and His agenda. It's time to recognize that the kingdom of God isn't an ethereal fairy tale located in a far-off land. It's both here and now.

That's our goal in this study.

*What ideas or images come to mind when you read or hear the phrase*
*kingdom of God?*

Before we move any further, let's establish two important definitions. First, the Bible refers to the kingdom of God as God's rule in this universe. His kingdom covers everything in creation and operates as a theocracy, where God rules, rather than a homocracy, where people rule. That's important.

With that in mind, let's use the Tony Evans Dictionary to define *kingdom of God:*

## KINGDOM OF GOD: GOD'S COMPREHENSIVE RULE OVER ALL CREATION

If God's kingdom is comprehensive, so is His kingdom agenda—His plan and program for the people and places under His dominion. So I define God's *kingdom agenda* as follows.

## KINGDOM AGENDA: THE VISIBLE DEMONSTRATION OF THE COMPREHENSIVE RULE OF GOD OVER EVERY AREA OF LIFE

We'll flesh out the practical elements of that definition in the days to come.

*What's your reaction to the previous definitions?*

The reason many believers are struggling is that we want God to bless our agendas instead of seeking to fulfill His kingdom agenda. We want God to OK our plans instead of seeking to fulfill His plans. We want God to bring us glory instead of seeking to bring Him glory.

But it doesn't work that way. God has only one plan: His kingdom agenda. That's why we'll spend this week exploring ways we can make sure we're following His plan instead of ours.

*Day 2*

# GOD'S KINGDOM AGENDA IS FROM ABOVE

Yesterday we defined God's *kingdom agenda* as the visible demonstration of the comprehensive rule of God over every area of life. To put things in more practical terms, God has a plan not just for your life and my life but for every facet of creation. He has a desired and designed program for everything contained in His kingdom.

The existence of this kingdom agenda has deep implications for all people because it offers us two distinct paths for how we choose to live our lives. We can get with the program and operate in submission to God's kingdom agenda, or we can go our own way and follow our own plans, goals, dreams, and desires.

People who choose their own path live in rebellion against God. By operating against God's kingdom, they create damaging consequences for individuals, for families, for churches, and for nations. We're currently experiencing these detrimental consequences throughout Western culture.

In contrast, people who choose to follow God's kingdom agenda live as active, productive members of God's kingdom. They experience the joy of fulfilling their purpose in life and of living in greater harmony with God.

During what seasons of life have you followed your own path and made your own choices rather than submitting to God's plan?

During what seasons of life have you intentionally followed God's plan rather than your own desires?

What outcomes did you experience in each of the previous seasons of life?

Our goal for this study is to understand the importance of relinquishing our agendas in order to follow God's plan and purposes for our lives. We also want to learn how we can intentionally and practically submit to God's blueprint rather than our own desires.

To move in those directions, we'll use the rest of this week to examine four fundamental truths about God's kingdom agenda:

1. GOD'S KINGDOM AGENDA IS NOT OF THIS WORLD.

2. GOD'S KINGDOM AGENDA REFLECTS HIS SOVEREIGNTY.

3. GOD'S KINGDOM AGENDA OPERATES FOR HIS GLORY.

4. GOD'S KINGDOM AGENDA OPERATES ACCORDING TO HIS WILL.

## NOT OF THIS WORLD

Before the crucifixion and resurrection, Jesus was forced to endure a series of interrogations by religious leaders and government officials, including the Roman governor, Pilate. Interestingly, Jesus used that conversation to deliver some of His clearest teachings on the kingdom of God.

The Jews wanted the Roman government to execute Jesus, so they accused Him of claiming to be an earthly king. Following that accusation, Pilate asked Jesus directly, "Are You the King of the Jews?" (John 18:33). Here's what happened next:

> *Jesus answered, "My kingdom is not of this world. If My kingdom were of this world, then My servants would be fighting so that I would not be handed over to the Jews; but as it is, My kingdom is not of this realm."*
> JOHN 18:36

Jesus' words highlight our first truth about the kingdom:

### GOD'S KINGDOM AGENDA IS NOT OF THIS WORLD.

Notice Jesus didn't say that His kingdom isn't *in* this world. Rather, He said His kingdom isn't *of* this world. His kingdom doesn't originate on earth; it originates in heaven. His kingdom has its source in the heavenlies, not in history. And because Jesus represented another King from another kingdom outside this world, He didn't resort to the methodologies of this world to defend Himself. He didn't rely on a physical army to rescue Him from death, because He was committed to a different agenda.

Why is this important? Because if you're a follower of Jesus, you also represent a kingdom that's not of this world. Therefore, to live your life according to God's kingdom agenda means many of your actions and decisions won't align with this world's professed wisdom and preferred methods.

In other words, you'll be different. You'll be noticed and called out by the people of this world because you're different. You may even experience persecution, as Jesus did.

What are some of the main purposes of life that our culture typically elevates and embraces? Record at least three.

1.

2.

3.

How do your main goals and purposes in life compare and contrast with the previous list?

## THE RIGHT PERSPECTIVE

When we understand that God's kingdom is not of this world, we realize that God's kingdom agenda must be carried out from the perspective of heaven, not of earth. That's why Jesus consistently made statements like this:

> *No one can serve two masters; for either he will hate the one and love the other,*
> *or he will be devoted to one and despise the other. You cannot serve God and*
> *wealth. For this reason I say to you, do not be worried about your life, as to what*
> *you will eat or what you will drink; nor for your body, as to what you will put*
> *on. Is not life more than food, and the body more than clothing? But seek first*
> *His kingdom and His righteousness, and all these things will be added to you.*
> MATTHEW 6:24-25,33

What's your initial reaction to these verses? Why?

Far too many Christians think they can mix a little of God with a lot of the world. They're willing to follow several isolated fragments of what they find in God's Word—going to church for fellowship, giving money when it's convenient, not committing murder, and so on—but they're not willing to submit to God's comprehensive plan and purpose for their lives. In other words, they're not willing to be part of His kingdom agenda.

That's a problem. Because when you bring the world into the Word, you're asking God, the King, to bless something that's contrary to His kingdom. He won't do that. In the end your efforts to keep hold of a little piece of God actually prevent you from experiencing any part of God. You can't operate in two kingdoms at once.

> In what areas of life are you attempting to mix God and the world in order to follow your own agenda?

I'll never forget the morning I got soap in my eyes while I was in the shower. My eyes started burning, so I tried to rub the soap out with my hand. But since my hand had soap on it, I only made things worse. Then I smacked my head against the soap dish while I was trying to grab a towel with my eyes closed, at the same time knocking the soap onto the bottom of the tub. And of course, the next instant I slipped on the soap and crashed onto the shower floor.

There I was, flailing around in the shower with a headache, a backache, and stinging eyes— all because something had blinded me and clouded my perspective.

Few things will be more counterproductive to your Christian walk than mixing earthly values with your perspective on life. It results in spiritual blindness. It keeps you from seeing what God wants you to see, which in turn keeps you from going where God wants you to go and doing what God wants you to do.

No, the only way to keep your vision clear is by viewing all of life through the perspective of God's kingdom agenda.

# GOD'S KINGDOM AGENDA
# REFLECTS HIS SOVEREIGNTY

I love it when visitors come to my house, so I often have friends over to talk, eat, or watch football. But there are certain rules I require people to follow when they enter my home.

For example, I don't allow any smoking inside my house. That doesn't mean I refuse to associate with people who smoke; it just means they have to snuff out their cigarettes or cigars before they walk through my front door. Similarly, I don't allow any profanity inside my house—not from my family members and not from visitors. So people who choose to swear need to do it somewhere else.

There have been some occasions where visitors have been unimpressed by the rules I've set up for my house, even upset. When that happens, I make it clear that guests are free to disagree with my line of thinking, but they have two choices about their status as visitors: they can stay at my house and follow my rules, or they can leave and do whatever they like somewhere else. Because it's my house.

What are some rules in your house that you consider important?

How do you typically respond when people break those rules?

Today we're going to focus on the second fundamental truth about God's kingdom agenda:

## GOD'S KINGDOM AGENDA REFLECTS HIS SOVEREIGNTY.

When you submit yourself to God's kingdom agenda, you place yourself under the King's sovereign rule. Because it's God's house.

What ideas or images come to mind when you hear the word *sovereignty?*

# GOD IS IN CHARGE

Sovereignty is a concept many people don't like or understand, especially when applied to God. But at the core, the fact that God is sovereign simply refers to His supremacy over all aspects of creation. His rules are universal, absolute, and comprehensive. Therefore, God is accountable to no one. He is sovereign.

Many passages of Scripture help us understand this aspect of God's character. Here's one:

> *The LORD has established His throne in the heavens,*
> *And His sovereignty rules over all.*
> PSALM 103:19

Read the following passages of Scripture and record what they teach about God's sovereignty.

1 Chronicles 29:11-12

Psalm 145:13

Ephesians 1:3-12

This world is God's house, and it operates according to His rules. That means unless you and I want to go out and create our own universe, we need to adjust to the rules of God's house or else prepare to suffer the consequences of our rebellion. Those are the only options before us.

But adjusting to the rules of God's house has major implications. To acknowledge God's sovereignty is to acknowledge His jurisdiction over every realm of life—including *your* life. To acknowledge His jurisdiction is to acknowledge the validity of His legislation in and over every area of your life. It's to align all your life under God's kingdom agenda.

Many Christians behave like teenagers in God's house. They say, "We're happy to live in Your place, God. We'll eat the food You provide. We'll enjoy the accommodations and other blessings You bring us. But we've got some of our own rules we need to follow. And we've got a few complaints we need to bring to Your attention."

In short, they want to experience the goodness of God's house without also submitting to God's rules—without recognizing God's sovereign authority. It just doesn't work that way.

How have your recent actions and attitudes reflected God's sovereignty over your life?

In what areas of life are you attempting to operate by your own rules?

Yes, living in God's kingdom brings blessings, but you don't get to enjoy the blessings of the King if you're not willing to live for His kingdom and under His sovereign authority. In other words, until you become a kingdom person who makes decisions based on God's kingdom agenda, you'll miss out on the abundant life He has in store for you.

## GOD IS IN CONTROL

God's sovereignty over His creation means He's in charge of all aspects of that creation. In the same way, the fact that God is sovereign means everything that happens in creation—including everything that happens in your life and mine—is either caused by God or allowed by God.

That's an important distinction. There are times when God actively causes things to happen in history. There are other times when we cause things to happen as people operating in our own free will, and yet nothing we attempt can actually come to pass unless God in His sovereignty allows it to happen.

This helps us answer the question, If God is sovereign, why is there so much chaos in the world? God's sovereignty doesn't mean there won't be any problems. It doesn't mean Satan won't rebel or people won't refuse to obey God's will.

What God's sovereignty does mean is that He's ultimately in control of every situation in this world. It means He will guide, direct, and ultimately use all things according to His kingdom agenda.

What's your response to the previous statements?

God's sovereignty means He's going to get wherever He's going. His kingdom agenda can't be thwarted, stopped, altered, or negated. That's why the apostle Paul wrote:

*We know that God causes all things to work together for good to those*
*who love God, to those who are called according to His purpose.*
ROMANS 8:28

What emotions do you experience when you read this verse? Why?

When has God caused difficult circumstances to "work together for good" in your life?

Paul was writing to committed Christians—those who "love God" and "are called according to His purpose." In other words, this verse applies only to people who are intentionally living according to God's kingdom agenda.

Now for the good news: God is in control of your life and all of your circumstances. Moreover, God is completely able to work in the different circumstances of your life to bring about good things according to His purposes.

Maybe you say, "But Tony, things are falling apart here! People are putting me down. I lost my job. The doctors say they don't know if I'm going to make it." I understand all that, and I've felt the pain you're experiencing in those kinds of situations. But the fact remains that God is sovereign over all things. Just because everything seems out of control, it's only out of *your* control—not God's.

What situations seem out of control in your life right now?

If life is difficult for you right now, don't approach God in His sovereignty with an attitude that says, "Lord, this is what I want." Rather, ask, "Lord, what do You want?" That's the question that defines a life lived according to God's kingdom agenda.

*Day 4*

# GOD'S KINGDOM AGENDA
# OPERATES FOR HIS GLORY

*Glory* is a common term in the Bible, one we usually encounter in connection with God. Unfortunately, we as Christians often miss the full meaning and significance of these encounters because our definition of *glory* has become skewed by the culture around us.

For example, people in our culture often make a connection between glory and fame or glory and riches. We see people on the covers of magazines and think, *They look glorious* or, *That person is covered in glory.* To be honest, we've confused glory with bling.

People in our culture also connect glory and victory—especially victory in sports or in warfare. How many movies have you seen in which Roman gladiators or historical generals shout for their followers to fight for glory? How many times have you heard sportswriters and announcers talk about an athlete's career in terms of glory?

These definitions of *glory* may be accepted in our cultural lexicon today, but they miss the mark when it comes to a biblical understanding of glory.

In what other ways have you seen *glory* defined or interpreted?

What ideas or images come to your mind when you hear the word *glory?*

So how are we to understand the concept of glory as it's presented in the Bible? We'll explore that today as we study the third fundamental truth about God's kingdom agenda:

GOD'S KINGDOM AGENDA OPERATES FOR HIS GLORY.

## CREATED FOR HIS GLORY

Let's begin exploring the connection between God's glory and His kingdom agenda by examining these powerful words by the apostle Paul:

*Oh, the depth of the riches both of the wisdom and knowledge of God! How*
*unsearchable are His judgments and unfathomable His ways! For who has*
*known the mind of the LORD, or who became His counselor? Or who has first*
*given to Him that it might be paid back to Him again? For from Him and*
*through Him and to Him are all things. To Him be the glory forever. Amen.*
ROMANS 11:33-36

What's your initial reaction to these verses? Why?

What do these verses teach you about God?

Notice the progression in verse 36. Paul described everything in creation as coming "from Him and through Him and to Him." In other words, everything that exists was created by God, is currently supported by God, and ultimately points to God. Moreover, none of this happens randomly. It all has a purpose, which Paul described this way: "To [God] be the glory forever."

So the reason God created the universe and everything in it—including you and me—was for His pleasure and His glory. Don't let anyone tell you that God created the world and people because He was lonely and needed companionship. That's false. God created this world and human beings for the primary purpose of displaying and reflecting His glory.

Look at the words of the prophet Isaiah:

*Bring My sons from afar*
*And My daughters from the ends of the earth,*
*Everyone who is called by My name,*
*And whom I have created for My glory,*
*Whom I have formed, even whom I have made.*
ISAIAH 43:6-7

You and I were created for the purpose of bringing God glory. That's a vital component of God's kingdom agenda for us.

## GLORY DEFINED

So what is glory? How do we understand glory when it's connected with God? In the New Testament the Greek word translated *glory* essentially means *to be heavy* or *to have weight*. This isn't physical weight, of course, but rather significance. The more glory something has, the heavier it becomes in terms of its importance.

That's not all. To fully comprehend the concept of God's glory, we need to understand the difference between ascribed glory and intrinsic glory. Most of us are familiar only with ascribed glory. This is the kind of glory we assign to people based on who they are or what they do. For example, judges carry ascribed glory when they put on their robes and everyone says, "Your Honor." When they lose the robes, they lose the glory. It's ascribed.

Human beings can carry only ascribed glory. But God is different. God's glory is intrinsic. His glory stays with Him at all times; it's part of Him.

> Read the following passages of Scripture and record what they teach about God's intrinsic glory.
>
> Exodus 33:15-23
>
> Ezekiel 1:22-28
>
> Matthew 24:29-31

Think of it this way: the sun doesn't try to be bright. It's always bright, even at night or on cloudy days when things seem dark to us. In the same way, God always exudes glory. He's eternally glorious. And just as the moon reflects the brightness of the sun, all creation has been designed to reflect God's glory and direct it back to Him—including you and me.

> How do we reflect glory back to God? What does that look like?

> When have you intentionally sought to glorify God in recent days? What happened?

## GOOD NEWS FOR US

God's glory has tremendous implications for those of us who submit ourselves to His kingdom agenda. Look at Colossians 1:15-17:

> *[Jesus] is the image of the invisible God, the firstborn of all creation. For by Him all things were created, both in the heavens and on earth, visible and invisible, whether thrones or dominions or rulers or authorities—all things have been created through Him and for Him. He is before all things, and in Him all things hold together.*
> COLOSSIANS 1:15-17

How do these verses contribute to your understanding of God's glory?

There's that same principle again: "All things have been created through Him and for Him" (v. 16). All creation has been designed by God for His glory. But look at that last phrase: "In Him all things hold together" (v. 17).

If you abide by and live according to God's kingdom agenda, Christ will bring together the things in your life that are falling apart. He will either fix the situation you're in, or He will fix *you* in the middle of that situation. He will hold things together for you, so fasten your eyes on Him when the going gets tough.

How do you need Jesus to hold things together for you right now?

But to receive the benefit of God's hand when things are falling apart, you must live your life for His glory. You must say, "Lord, my goal today is to reflect Your significance. I want to ascribe to You the glory that already belongs to You. I want to radiate, demonstrate, magnify, and illustrate Your glory."

That's what it means to live as part of God's kingdom agenda.

# GOD'S KINGDOM AGENDA OPERATES ACCORDING TO HIS WILL

When I was a little boy growing up in Baltimore, one of the first toys I remember playing with was a little jack-in-the-box. When I wound up the crank on the side of the box, it played the tune "Pop Goes the Weasel." I'd keep winding and winding, of course, building up the tension until boom! A spring was activated somewhere in the box, and a painted clown popped out of the top. I loved that toy. It always scared me a little, but I still loved it.

The concept of a jack-in-the-box is great for a toy but not so great for God. Yet so many people today, even a number of Christians, treat God as if He were a clown they can call up whenever they need Him and then stuff back in the box again when they want to go back to their own way of life.

That brings us to the fourth and final truth we need to explore about God's kingdom agenda. So far we've seen that God's kingdom agenda originates in heaven, reflects God's sovereignty, and operates for His glory. Today we'll explore this kingdom principle:

### GOD'S KINGDOM AGENDA OPERATES ACCORDING TO HIS WILL.

What ideas or images come to mind when you hear phrases such as "God's will" or "the will of God"?

## GOD'S KINGDOM WILL

Let's continue our exploration of God's kingdom agenda by focusing on Daniel 7, which records a supernatural vision that God gave to the prophet Daniel. That vision contained powerful images and prophecies that were overwhelming to Daniel at the time; he wasn't able to comprehend the full scope of what he saw. Looking back from our perspective, however, we can see that God blessed His prophet with an accurate picture and prediction of several future kingdoms that would rule on earth.

Read Daniel 7:1-12. Which images are emphasized most in Daniel's vision?

Daniel envisioned four beasts: a lion with eagle's wings, a bear, a leopard, and a terrifying beast of unknown form. These four beasts corresponded to four specific kingdoms or nations in history. The lion represented the Babylonian Empire. The bear represented the Medo-Persian Empire. The leopard represented the Greek Empire led by Alexander the Great. And the terrifying beast represented the Roman Empire and its many offshoots.

Essentially, Daniel saw a prophetic vision of actual historical kingdoms that would come to power on earth. But that's not all. After his vision of earthly kingdoms, Daniel also received fascinating insight into God's heavenly kingdom:

> *I kept looking in the night visions,*
> *And behold, with the clouds of heaven*
> *One like a Son of Man was coming,*
> *And He came up to the Ancient of Days*
> *And was presented before Him.*
> ***And to Him was given dominion,***
> ***Glory and a kingdom,***
> *That all the peoples, nations and men of every language*
> *Might serve Him.*
> *His dominion is an everlasting dominion*
> *Which will not pass away;*
> *And His kingdom is one*
> *Which will not be destroyed.*
> DANIEL 7:13-14, emphasis added

How do these verses enhance your understanding of God's kingdom?

Notice the progression in these verses. First, "One like a Son of Man was coming" (v. 13)—that's Jesus. Son of Man was a messianic title used several places in Scripture. Jesus specifically used this title to describe Himself in the Gospels.

Next we have the "Ancient of Days" (v. 13)—that's God—deliberately giving dominion, glory, and a kingdom to Jesus (see v. 14). This was a symbolic representation of the fact that Jesus is the driving force in God's kingdom and has the authority to carry out God's kingdom agenda. In other words, Jesus is in control.

Finally, we see our part in this huge, heavenly picture:

> *That all the peoples, nations and men of every language*
> *Might serve Him.*
> DANIEL 7:14

Do you see the connection? Jesus has been given glory and dominion over God's kingdom, and we've been charged to reflect that glory and serve Him in all things.

In other words, you and I were brought into God's kingdom to serve Christ and to do His will. That's the goal we should strive for every day.

How have you intentionally served Jesus in recent days?

What we need to understand is that God's kingdom is moving forward, whether or not we're on board. His kingdom agenda can't be stopped. His plans can't be thwarted or delayed. God has said:

> *As the heavens are higher than the earth,*
> *So are My ways higher than your ways*
> *And My thoughts than your thoughts.*
> *For as the rain and the snow come down from heaven,*
> *And do not return there without watering the earth*
> *And making it bear and sprout,*
> *And furnishing seed to the sower and bread to the eater;*
> *So will My word be which goes forth from My mouth;*
> *It will not return to Me empty,*
> *Without accomplishing what I desire,*
> *And without succeeding in the matter for which I sent it.*
> ISAIAH 55:9-11

It's our job, as members of God's kingdom, to set aside our plans and desires, submit to His kingdom will, and work to carry out His kingdom agenda.

Jesus Himself modeled this principle for us when confronted with His own crucifixion, the most painful, humiliating experience imaginable:

*He withdrew from them about a stone's throw, and He knelt down*
*and began to pray, saying, "Father, if You are willing, remove*
*this cup from Me; yet not My will, but Yours be done."*
LUKE 22:41-42

What obstacles regularly prevent you from identifying God's will?

What obstacles regularly hinder you from carrying out God's will?

How can these obstacles be overcome?

## BECOMING A KINGDOM PERSON

Do you want to be a kingdom person? Do you want to discover God's plan for your life—the place and work He has for you in His kingdom agenda? It doesn't have to be a mystery. God is both willing and waiting to reveal it to you. But you must come to the place of submission to His will. If you don't know how to find that place, ask God to show you the way. Seek Him by restructuring your thoughts, words, and actions to conform to the standards of His kingdom.

Again, Jesus is not only the authority in God's kingdom but also our example for living each day according to God's kingdom agenda. For example, look at His words in what we refer to as the Lord's Prayer:

*Pray, then, in this way:*
*"Our Father who is in heaven,*
*Hallowed be Your name.*
*Your kingdom come.*
*Your will be done,*
*On earth as it is in heaven.*
*Give us this day our daily bread.*
*And forgive us our debts, as we also have forgiven our debtors.*
*And do not lead us into temptation, but deliver us from evil.*
*For Yours is the kingdom and the power and the glory forever. Amen."*
MATTHEW 6:9-13

What do you like best about Jesus' prayer? Why?

How does this prayer compare to the way you normally pray?

Notice that Jesus' prayer begins with a desire to exalt God's name—to proclaim God as unique and worthy of all honor in creation (see v. 9). Also notice the posture of humility Jesus took before His Father:

> *Your kingdom come.*
> *Your will be done,*
> *On earth as it is in heaven.*
> MATTHEW 6:10

Finally, notice how that humility shaped the end of Jesus' prayer: "Yours is the kingdom and the power and the glory forever" (v. 13). Jesus was showing us how to bend our wills in submission to God's will. He was demonstrating the necessity of letting go of our earthly kingdoms and desires in order to grab hold of God's kingdom agenda.

I can't tell you everything that following God's kingdom agenda will mean for you on a practical level. I just know that whatever it is, you must be willing to do His will, not your own. You must be able to pray, "Your will be done" and "Yours is the kingdom and the power and the glory forever" (vv. 10,13).

How will you intentionally submit to God's will this week?

In the days and weeks to follow, I want to challenge you to live your life according to God's kingdom agenda—to submit to your King and seek His kingdom. God is the source of all things. He's in charge. He's sovereign. He's your Lord and mine. And when you do His will, you become His representative in a world that longs to find a better way to live.

Week 2

# ONE LIFE UNDER GOD

## START

**Welcome back to this small-group discussion of** Kingdom Agenda.

The previous session's application challenge encouraged you to be aware of the moments during the week when your status as a member of God's kingdom clashed with your daily participation in modern culture. If you're comfortable, share what you experienced or what insights you gained.

Describe what you liked best in the material from week 1. What questions do you have?

What values and standards distinguish a kingdom person from someone who's living according to his or her own values and standards?

What ideas or images come to mind when you hear the word *purpose?*

To prepare for the DVD segment, read aloud the following verses.

*We preach to you the good news of the promise made to the fathers, that God has fulfilled this promise to our children in that He raised up Jesus, as it is also written in the second Psalm, "You are My Son; today I have begottn You." As for the fact that He raised Him up from the dead, no longer to return to decay, He has spoken in this way: "I will give you the holy and sure blessings of David." Therefore He also says in another Psalm, "You will not allow Your Holy One to undergo decay." For David, after he had served the purpose of God in his own generation, fell asleep, and was laid among his fathers and underwent decay; but He whom God raised did not undergo decay.*
ACTS 13:32-37

# WATCH

**Complete the viewer guide below as you watch DVD session 2.**

God created you for His _____.

God has given you a _____—a divinely ordained mission in life.

David served the _____ of God (see Acts 13:36).

People are living for _____ and missing the purpose of God for which God's kingdom has both redeemed and called them.

The calling or purpose God has designated for you becomes an _____ to draw others into the kingdom.

When you discover that God has a _____ for you in His kingdom, it changes everything.

David impacted his _____ (see Acts 13:36).

You've been called for a purpose: the _____ of God through the expansion of His kingdom while it impacts _____.

**Finding Your Calling**

1. Your purpose will always involve your _____.

2. Your calling involves your _____.

3. Your calling involves your _____.

4. God creates _____.

David fell _____ (see Acts 13:36).

If you are not living for the purpose, you're missing the _____.
And if you're missing the kingdom, you will not see all that the King has provided for you.

# RESPOND

*Use the following questions to discuss the DVD segment with your group.*

What did you appreciate most in Dr. Evans's teaching? Why?

Where does our culture typically turn when searching for meaning and purpose in life?

Respond to Dr. Evans's definition of *calling:* "a divinely ordained mission in life which you are equipped, empowered, and ordained to fulfill so that God is glorified and His kingdom is expanded."

What are some of your primary passions in life? What are the main abilities God has blessed you with?

How would you summarize your calling in life?

How confident are you that the current trajectory of your life is aligned with the purpose and calling God has for you? Explain.

What barriers or obstacles have prevented you from fully experiencing your divine calling as a member of God's kingdom?

**Application.** Spend time this week actively contemplating your God-given calling and purpose in life. Make a note of moments when you feel passionate about an idea or a cause. Also make a note of times when you feel fulfilled in using your God-given talents and abilities to accomplish something meaningful.

**This week's Scripture memory.**

> *Seek first His kingdom and His righteousness, and all these things will be added to you.*
> MATTHEW 6:33

**Assignment.** Read week 2 and complete the activities before the next group experience.

## TOUCHING FIRST BASE

Baseball has been an important part of American life for more than a century—and for good reason. There's something unique about sitting at the ballpark, cheering for each batter, grabbing a hot dog (or two), watching for foul balls, and standing for the seventh-inning stretch.

It helps that the game itself is relatively easy to understand. The pitcher throws the ball, each batter tries to hit the ball, and then those batters try to make their way around four separate bases and score a run before the defense can stop them. There's an intuitive quality to the game that almost anyone can grasp.

One of the most important principles of baseball is that, as a batter, you must reach first base after getting a hit in order to score a run. If you miss first base, nothing else you do will count. It doesn't matter if you've hit the ball to the outfield wall, it doesn't matter if you touch home plate, and it doesn't matter if the crowd goes wild cheering you. Touching first base is a necessary step if you want to accomplish anything else.

Keep that image of first base in your mind, because we're going to cover a lot of ground in this study. We're going to talk about how God's kingdom agenda should influence your family, your church, your community, and even your nation. But none of that will matter if you miss first base—the way God's kingdom agenda should influence you as an individual.

That's our focus this week: your life as an individual citizen of God's kingdom. What does it mean to live as a man or a woman who attempts to follow God's kingdom agenda?

We'll answer that question by exploring a number of different aspects of your life: your priorities, your purpose and calling, your responsibilities, and your spiritual growth. But throughout these discussions I want you to remember that image of touching first base. Because if you miss the implications of God's kingdom agenda for you as an individual, you won't be able to accomplish anything of eternal value in this life.

*Day 1*

# YOUR KINGDOM PRIORITIES

There was once a man who visited the doctor because, as he put it, "Everything hurts." He told the doctor his entire body was in agony. Every place he touched, from his head to his toes, produced great pain.

At first the doctor was stumped. He looked the man over and couldn't find anything wrong. He hooked the man to different machines and performed several tests, but everything came up normal; the man seemed to be in perfect health. And yet the doctor observed that the man cried out in pain anytime he touched any part of his own body.

Eventually the doctor figured it out. With a sigh he said, "Sir, it seems you've dislocated your finger."

The man was certainly in pain, but what he believed to be a multitude of injuries covering his entire body turned out to be just one problem: his finger. This was good news, because if the man could fix that one problem—if he could get his finger back in line—then all the pain he thought he was experiencing in the other areas of his body would be fixed as well.

> What are some painful areas in your life right now—physical or otherwise? What's causing you discomfort or agony?

> How do you typically respond to pain and difficult circumstances?

A lot of people in this world, including a number of Christians, are carrying a great deal of pain, disappointment, and frustration as they make their way through life. Maybe you've felt that way. Maybe even now you can relate to the idea that everything hurts.

If so, I've got good news for you. It's very possible that your entire life isn't in shambles, even if it seems that way. The pain you're experiencing is real, but I doubt your entire life is out of whack.

Instead, chances are good that you're simply suffering from dislocated priorities. And if you're able to fix that one problem, everything else will fall into place.

## SEEK FIRST

The longest of Jesus' sermons recorded in the Bible is often called the Sermon on the Mount. This sermon, spanning three chapters in God's Word (see Matt. 5–7), was originally addressed to believers—specifically Jesus' disciples. Therefore, Jesus' Sermon on the Mount is primarily a sermon about God's kingdom.

The centerpiece of the Sermon on the Mount is found in one verse. In fact, this one verse is the key to living as a member of God's kingdom:

> *Seek first His kingdom and His righteousness, and all these things will be added to you.*
> MATTHEW 6:33

What's your initial reaction to this verse? Why?

The word I want you to focus on is *first:* "Seek *first* His kingdom and His righteousness." As individual Christians living in God's kingdom, we need to understand that we must prioritize God's kingdom agenda. We must seek His agenda first before we seek to accomplish anything else or fulfill any other desire.

To live life to its fullest and to accomplish and experience all God has created you to do, you must first seek God and His kingdom agenda. God isn't willing to be one influence or one priority among many in your life. He must be first and foremost. That truth is a key component of what it means to live as a man or a woman in God's kingdom.

What ideas or images come to mind when you hear the word *priority?*

How do you typically set priorities for your everyday activities?

How do you typically set priorities for your long-term goals and plans?

This concept of first seeking God's kingdom and His kingdom agenda isn't limited to the Sermon on the Mount. Rather, it's a central theme throughout God's Word.

For example, Deuteronomy 6:4-9 has served as one of the most important passages of Scripture for the Jewish community from the time of Moses until today. Often referred to as the Shema, these verses highlight God's place as the central and primary priority for all walks of life:

> *Hear, O Israel! The LORD is our God, the LORD is one! You shall love the LORD*
> *your God with all your heart and with all your soul and with all your might.*
> *These words, which I am commanding you today, shall be on your heart. You shall*
> *teach them diligently to your sons and shall talk of them when you sit in your house*
> *and when you walk by the way and when you lie down and when you rise up.*
> *You shall bind them as a sign on your hand and they shall be as frontals on your*
> *forehead. You shall write them on the doorposts of your house and on your gates.*
> DEUTERONOMY 6:4-9

What emotions do you experience when you read these verses?

How do these verses emphasize the importance of first seeking God and His kingdom?

The New Testament also makes it clear that living as part of God's kingdom means giving first priority to God and His kingdom agenda. For example, look at these words by the apostle Paul:

> *[Christ] is before all things, and in Him all things hold together. He is also*
> *head of the body, the church; and He is the beginning, the firstborn from the*
> *dead, **so that He Himself will come to have first place in everything.***
> COLOSSIANS 1:17-18, emphasis added

I often hear people tell me they just don't have time for God. That's sad. It's also untrue. What those people are really telling me is that God doesn't have first place in their lives—that they haven't prioritized His kingdom agenda. Because we as human beings always have time for what we value most. We always make room for our top priority.

For what people and activities do you intentionally make time?

How have you intentionally made time for God and His kingdom in recent days or weeks?

So how do we know if we're properly prioritizing God and His kingdom agenda? What does that look like? One of the best ways to evaluate whether you're putting God first in your life is to ask yourself this question: *Where do I turn when I need to make a decision?*

When a problem arises in your life, do you first turn to other people for guidance? Is your first step to evaluate potential solutions based on your past experience and present knowledge? Or do you turn to God? Do you make decisions based primarily on your goals and desires or on God's?

Where do you typically turn when you need to make a decision?

What does your answer to the previous question reveal about your priorities in life?

When the God you claim to acknowledge isn't treated as God, you won't find the benefits you seek from His kingdom. The key to kingdom success is that critical word *first:* "Seek first His kingdom and His righteousness" (Matt. 6:33).

## FIND WHAT YOU NEED

Don't miss the second part of that pivotal statement in Matthew 6:33. When you first seek God's kingdom agenda, "all these things will be added to you." That's a provocative statement, isn't it? What things? What will be added to us when we seek the kingdom first? Let's get a little more context from Matthew 6.

Read Matthew 6:25-34. What are the main benefits or desirable things mentioned in these verses?

Specifically look for the words *worry* and *worried.* What do these verses teach about anxiety?

Worry is one of the habits we fall into most easily as human beings. We worry about money. We worry about our clothes and our appearance. We worry about our food. And sometimes we worry about what our food is doing to our clothes and our appearance. We're naturals when it comes to anxiety.

What are the main causes of anxiety in your life?

Because of our natural tendency to worry, it's fascinating that one of the biggest benefits of first seeking God and His kingdom agenda is that we get to let go of our worry and anxiety. God has promised that when we prioritize Him, we'll find what we need.

I want to challenge you today to change one thing about your current life. Then watch as that one thing transforms everything else in your life. Make God your first priority. Make Him first in your thoughts, hopes, and decisions. Place Him at the forefront of the way you spend your time and interact with the world around you. Place Him first. Honor Him first. Give to Him first.

Because when you "seek first His kingdom and His righteousness" (Matt. 6:33), when you give priority to His kingdom agenda, everything else will fall into place.

Identify one change you'll make this week to place God and His kingdom first in your life.

*Day 2*

# YOUR KINGDOM IDENTITY

We're focusing this week on what it means to live as individuals in God's kingdom—on how we should operate as men and women who seek to follow God's kingdom agenda in the many aspects of our personal lives. In light of that focus, I think it's important that we understand who we are as followers of Christ—as kingdom citizens.

Let's get started with a little exercise. Answer the following questions, but don't reference your name, your job title, or your family. Give it a try.

Who are you?

What do you do?

The way you answered those questions says a lot about you and especially about your knowledge of who you really are.

In the early church the people who responded to the gospel message were dead serious about living as followers of Christ. In fact, the early Christians were known throughout their culture as people of "the Way" (Acts 19:9) because they'd chosen to walk a new and completely different path in life. Those early believers lived for God's kingdom and based their entire identities on His kingdom agenda.

A great tragedy in the church today is that many Christians identify their faith as just another addition to their personal portfolios. Following Christ is a part of who they are and what they do. You can see this in the way people write autobiographies for their blogs or social-media accounts that say, "I'm a manager at this company, I've been married for 15 years, I'm a Christian, and I love watching football" or "I've got three kids, I enjoy these hobbies, and I go to church."

What does your bio say on your website or social-media accounts?

Let me be frank: if you've recently been introduced to someone and conversed with that person for more than a minute without bringing up God or His kingdom, you're a confused Christian. As a member of God's kingdom, your identity should be entirely wrapped up with Christ. It should be impossible for you to talk at any length about yourself without talking about Him.

What's your response to the previous statements?

The reason I feel strongly about this point is that you and I must understand our basic identity as disciples of Jesus Christ in order to cultivate a kingdom mentality for our personal lives and to experience the spiritual growth God intends for us.

## OUR IDENTITY

*Disciple* is a great term for us to focus on as we contemplate our identity as members of God's kingdom. To be a Christian is to live as a disciple of Jesus Christ.

What ideas or images come to mind when you hear the word *disciple?*

How would you summarize the role of a disciple in your own words?

The Greek word translated *disciple* in the New Testament essentially means *learner.* It refers to a student who follows the teachings, behaviors, and practices of another person so closely, so intensely that the student becomes a clone of the teacher. We could also think of a disciple as an apprentice—someone who works alongside a master tradesman to learn the skills for practicing that trade.

Jesus referred to that type of relationship when He instructed His first disciples:

*A disciple is not above his teacher, nor a slave above his master. It is enough*
*for the disciple that he become like his teacher, and the slave like his master.*
MATTHEW 10:24-25

So one of our primary goals as disciples of Jesus is to become like Him—to pattern our lives after His and to follow Him so closely that we think, speak, and act like Him.

Read the following passages of Scripture and record what they teach about living as a disciple of Christ.

Luke 14:25-33

John 8:31-32

John 13:34-35

What additional practices have helped you become more like Christ?

## OUR COMMISSION TO MAKE DISCIPLES

We can't talk about living as disciples of Jesus without mentioning the Great Commission. Among Jesus' last recorded words on earth, these verses serve as His charge and challenge to any of us who choose to live as members of His kingdom:

*Jesus came up and spoke to them, saying, "All authority has been given to Me in heaven*
*and on earth. Go therefore and make disciples of all the nations, baptizing them in*
*the name of the Father and the Son and the Holy Spirit, teaching them to observe all*
*that I commanded you; and lo, I am with you always, even to the end of the age."*
MATTHEW 28:18-20

Notice two aspects of Jesus' commission:

1. We're commanded as disciples to make more disciples.

2. We're commanded as disciples to embrace the process of spiritual growth.

"Go therefore and make disciples of all the nations" (v. 19). These are challenging words, not because we find them difficult to understand but because we often find them difficult to carry out.

I know too many Christians who attempt to ignore or shrug off their responsibility to make disciples of Jesus. They say, "I'm not gifted in evangelism." They say, "I feel I'm called to serve God in other areas." They say, "I'm working to live as a good example to the people around me, but I just haven't had any opportunities yet to share the gospel."

Those are excuses. Those are evasions. Jesus' command is clear: "Make disciples" (v. 19).

> What does it mean to make disciples in today's culture?

> How have you recently invested your time, your money, or your energy in making disciples?

## OUR COMMISSION TO GROW SPIRITUALLY

The first command in Jesus' Great Commission is to make disciples. The second command is to "[baptize] them in the name of the Father and the Son and the Holy Spirit, teaching them to observe all that I commanded" (vv. 19-20).

In other words, Jesus commands His followers to help new disciples walk through the process of spiritual growth as we ourselves grow spiritually.

> What ideas or images come to mind when you hear the phrase *spiritual growth?* Why?

It's not enough for us simply to baptize new believers into God's kingdom. That's not what Jesus meant when He said to make disciples. We need to go further. We need to teach them to observe all Jesus commanded. Of course, we can't teach others how to obey what Jesus commanded if we're not obeying what Jesus commanded in our own lives.

In other words, we have a commission to grow spiritually as we fulfill Jesus' command to help others growth spiritually.

In what ways have you experienced spiritual growth in recent years?

What obstacles have you overcome in order to experience that growth?

What obstacles are currently preventing your spiritual growth?

Remember earlier when we said our goal as disciples is to become like Jesus? Understand that a process is involved. It's not something that happens all at once. Rather, our lives as disciples of Christ should be marked by steady maturation and gradual transformation into the image of Christ (see 2 Cor. 3:18).

Therefore, don't be discouraged if you're not as mature as you want to be as a follower of Jesus. Don't get down on yourself for struggling—for having setbacks and failures and frustrations. Those are natural. Those are part of the process.

This is the question you need to ask yourself: *Am I closer to Christ today than I was a year ago?* If you can answer yes to that question, then you're growing; you're maturing as a disciple of Christ. If your answer is no, you need to address the obstacles in your life that have stunted the process of spiritual growth.

Are you closer to Christ today than you were a year ago? Explain.

A primary key to thriving in God's kingdom is to understand your identity as a disciple of Christ—and to act accordingly. May that be so in your life.

# YOUR KINGDOM CALLING

Have you ever suffered from same-ole disease? That's not an illness you'll find in a medical textbook. But as a pastor, I often encounter this sickness in the lives of those who come to me for spiritual guidance.

When you have same-ole disease, you wake up every morning and get out of the same-ole bed. You go to the same-ole bathroom and look in the same-ole mirror at the same-ole face. You go to the same-ole closet to choose from those same-ole clothes.

Then you go to the same-ole table to eat the same-ole breakfast. You get up and walk to the same-ole garage, get in the same-ole car, head down the same-ole road to arrive at the same-ole job. Once there, you do the same-ole work for the same-ole pay.

At the end of the day, you head back down the same-ole road, pull into the same-ole garage, and walk into the same-ole house. You sit down in the same-ole chair to watch those same-ole programs on the same-ole television. Or you surf the same-ole Internet.

At dinnertime you pull up to the same-ole table and eat the same-ole dinner again from those same-ole dishes. Then you fall into the same-ole bed so that you can wake up the next day and start the same-ole routine again.

> When have you suffered from same-ole disease?

> What makes you feel stuck in a rut or dissatisfied with your current experiences in life?

Too many Christians are living their lives without a sense of purpose. They're settling for an existence totally defined by the limits of their houses and jobs and cars and churches. But when we as followers of Christ settle for that kind of life, we miss God's reason for redeeming us and positioning us here on earth.

In other words, we miss our kingdom calling.

## DEFINING THE CALL

Have you ever felt you needed a little caffeine in your Christian cup? I have. I've been through seasons of life when things seemed to drag along day after day, as if I were in a rut. I've had times at work, at church, and at home when I wondered, *Where's the adventure in this? Where are the thrill and satisfaction that are supposed to come with serving the Creator of the universe?*

In each of those situations, what I ultimately discovered was that I needed clarity in my calling. I needed to refocus my life on the purpose God created me to fulfill, according to His kingdom agenda.

What purpose are you currently trying to fulfill in life?

When have you most strongly felt that you were living the kind of life God created you to live?

Make no mistake: there's adventure to be had in God's kingdom agenda. There's energy. There's life. There are fulfillment and satisfaction. But you'll experience those sensations only when you know and pursue your divine calling.

When you live out your God-given purpose—when you fulfill your destiny as defined by God's kingdom agenda—you'll experience God's energizing, eternally significant power to leverage your gifts and maximize your life's fullest potential.

Let's nail down a definition before we go any further. This is from the Tony Evans Dictionary, of course:

**CALLING:** THE CUSTOMIZED LIFE PURPOSE GOD HAS ORDAINED AND EQUIPPED YOU TO ACCOMPLISH IN ORDER TO BRING HIM THE GREATEST GLORY AND ACHIEVE THE MAXIMUM EXPANSION OF HIS KINGDOM

Based on this definition, how would you describe your calling in life?

Notice that a divine calling is always intended to bring about God's glory—to fulfill His kingdom agenda. Therefore, to follow your calling is to live in such a way that God's kingdom is put on display for all to see.

That's what Jesus had in mind when He talked about our responsibility to live as examples of God's kingdom and glory:

> *You are the light of the world. A city set on a hill cannot be hidden; nor does anyone light a lamp and put it under a basket, but on the lampstand, and it gives light to all who are in the house. Let your light shine before men in such a way that they may see your good works, and glorify your Father who is in heaven.*
> MATTHEW 5:14-16

What does it look like to "let your light shine before men" (v. 16)?

When have you recently been tempted to put your lamp under a basket? What happened?

As a child of the King, you're called to reflect Him and His kingdom through your specific purpose in life, and you're called to do so in such a remarkable fashion that people want to know more about the kingdom you represent. That's your destiny. That's your purpose. And if you're not representing God's kingdom in that way, don't be surprised when your life feels meaningless. Because it is.

## EXPLORING THE CALL

Now that we've defined your calling in life, let's explore several aspects of God's divine calling that will help you flesh out that definition in your life.

## 1. YOU RECEIVE YOUR CALLING FROM GOD ONLY AFTER YOU RESPOND TO THE PERSON OF GOD. That's because you need

to be in a relationship with God to hear and understand His calling. In other words, you must be part of God's kingdom before you get access to His kingdom agenda for your life.

It's not enough to say, "Lord, show me my calling" when you don't have a relationship with Him. If you don't relate to His Person, God won't trust you with His program.

How do you feel about your relationship with God?

Here's a good example of what I mean. After Jesus miraculously fed five thousand men with only a couple of fish and some loaves of bread, the people wanted to get on board with His program. They wanted to know how to be on Jesus' side so that they could get more free food. But look what happened next:

> *They said to Him, "What shall we do, so that we may work the*
> *works of God?" Jesus answered and said to them, "This is the work*
> *of God, that you believe in Him whom He has sent."*
> JOHN 6:28-29

The relationship must come first. God wants a relationship with you before He will bless you with the knowledge of your divine calling.

What steps can you take in the short term to improve your relationship with God? In the long term?

## 2. YOUR DIVINE CALLING IS CUSTOMIZED BY GOD. When

God reveals His plan and purpose for your life, it will be uniquely designed for your specific attributes and your specific situation. After all, you're unique; you're custom-made. Therefore, your calling will be unique—intentionally designed for you.

That's why Philippians 2:12 says, "Work out your salvation with fear and trembling." You're called to focus on *your* salvation and *your* calling, not somebody else's.

This means you don't have to try to be somebody else as a follower of Jesus. You don't have to acquire as much Bible knowledge as that scholar in your Bible-study group. You don't have to give as much money as a certain person in your church. You don't have to sing like anyone else, speak like anyone else, or act like anyone else. You can be yourself. God's calling is customized just for you.

What's your response to the previous statements?

When are you tempted to imitate others in the church?

## 3. GOD'S DIVINE CALLING REQUIRES A PERSONAL COMMITMENT FROM YOU. God will call you by name, and He will demand all of you—everything you are and everything you have—to connect your calling with His kingdom agenda.

That's why Paul used such extreme terms to describe his participation in God's kingdom:

*I have been crucified with Christ; and it is no longer I who live, but Christ lives in me; and the life which I now live in the flesh I live by faith in the Son of God, who loved me and gave Himself up for me.*
GALATIANS 2:20

In what ways have you willingly sacrificed your life to God?

In what ways are you still holding back and seeking control of your actions and attitudes?

As a member of God's kingdom, you don't have to settle for a mundane life. Rather, you have a divine calling from the Creator of the universe to glorify Him through your life and to advance His kingdom agenda.

# HOW TO FIND YOUR CALLING

I remember the moment when I first caught a clear, undeniable sense of God's calling for my life. As a young man, I was frequently preoccupied with football—so much so that those who knew me as a teenager might say my life revolved around the sport. I was involved with other activities in school and at church, but football was the thing that really mattered to me. It was my identity.

One particular evening, however, I found myself at an evangelistic crusade led by B. Sam Hart in a nearby town. Things happened so fast that I can hardly remember the details. It seemed one minute I was sitting in my chair preparing to hear the message, and the next minute I was on my knees under the tent praying, "God, what do You want me to do for You with the rest of my life?"

I was already a Christian at that point. I was under the godly influence of my father and other Bible teachers, and I'd even chosen to serve God in different ways at church—when I wasn't busy with football.

But I had a new experience with God that day—one of the most extraordinary experiences of my life. God found me under that tent and singled me out by name. He didn't reveal all of the details right away, but I knew without a doubt that He was calling me into His service for the remainder of my time on earth. I've never looked back.

How has your life been changed by meaningful encounters with God?

When have you recently felt God directing you to make specific decisions or follow a certain path?

Yesterday we explored the concept of divine calling. We saw that God has ordained and equipped us for a customized life purpose that's designed to bring Him the greatest glory and to achieve the maximum expansion of His kingdom.

Today I want to answer the next logical question: How do you and I find the divine calling God has for us?

## SEARCH FOR GOD

Let's get something clear right off the bat. If you want to know your calling in life, don't go looking for your calling in life. Rather, go looking for God. That's because God is the source of your calling and the only One who can lead you to your calling.

In many ways this pursuit becomes a test of your faith. Do you believe God knows where He wants you in this world? Do you believe God understands how you fit into His kingdom? Do you believe God is willing to communicate with you about your place in His kingdom agenda and what He wants you to accomplish? If so, then seek Him.

What are your answers to the previous questions?

What steps have you recently taken to seek God?

A foundational step in identifying your calling is to realize that God is the One who calls, and you're the one who's called. God is the Creator, and you're His creation. Therefore, you can never discover your calling in creation apart from the One who created you.

Moses is the biblical character who best exemplifies this principle. As a man in the prime of his life, he understood that God had called him to deliver the Israelites from their oppression and slavery in Egypt (see Acts 7:25). Unfortunately, Moses messed up. He attempted to fulfill his calling by murdering an Egyptian soldier—an action that was out-side God's will. As a result, Moses had to flee from Egypt and settle in the land of Midian (see Ex. 2:11-15).

After spending 40 years in the wilderness babysitting sheep, Moses was as far away from his calling as he could get. Things looked bleak. But then something incredible happened: Moses had an encounter with God.

Read Exodus 3:1-10. What's your initial reaction to these verses?

Notice what happened in verse 1:

> *Moses was pasturing the flock of Jethro his father-in-law, the priest of Midian; and he*
> *led the flock to the west side of the wilderness and came to Horeb, the mountain of God.*
> EXODUS 3:1

Moses had a supernatural experience with God and was ultimately reconnected with his divine calling after 40 years of waiting in the wilderness. And why did it happen? Because he made his way to where God was hanging out. He went into God's presence.

The same principle applies to you. If you want to know your calling, you have to go where God is. If you never spend time in God's presence, you'll never find your calling. If you never read and meditate on God's Word, you'll never find your calling. It's that simple.

What obstacles commonly prevent you from intentionally placing yourself in God's presence?

How can you overcome these obstacles?

## COMMIT TO GOD'S WILL

The second truth you need to understand as you seek to identify your calling is that God reveals His will only to those who are willing to obey His will and have committed to do so. In other words, you must submit to follow God's purpose for your life before He will reveal that purpose to you.

Look at what the apostle Paul had to say on this subject:

> *I urge you, brethren, by the mercies of God, to present your bodies a living and holy*
> *sacrifice, acceptable to God, which is your spiritual service of worship. And do not be*
> *conformed to this world, but be transformed by the renewing of your mind, so that you*
> *may prove what the will of God is, that which is good and acceptable and perfect.*
> ROMANS 12:1-2

Do you see the progression in these verses? First, present yourself as a sacrifice to God. Second, refuse to be conformed to the actions and attitudes of this world. Then, third, you will have opportunities to know and prove God's perfect will.

Too many Christians today say, "God, show me what You want me to do, and I'll let You know whether I'm on board. Please tell me Your plan for my life, and then I'll tell You whether I plan to follow it."

No. God's plans are not up for negotiation—including His divine call for your life. Understand that God will reveal your calling to you only when you reveal ahead of time that you're willing to obey.

Are you willing to follow God's divine calling for your life? Explain.

How have you expressed your commitment to God?

Totally giving yourself to God means giving Him full power over your life. When you submit to the King, you'll receive and understand your calling to His kingdom agenda.

# STEWARDSHIP IN GOD'S KINGDOM

When I was in seminary, one way my wife and I were able to manage on a tight budget was to house-sit for wealthy families in north Dallas. When these wealthy families went on vacations for extended periods of time, they often contacted seminaries in search of trustworthy people to watch their houses while they were gone.

As students, we always coveted these opportunities for two reasons: they provided a source of income, and they gave us a chance to manage houses, appliances, furniture, food, and even cars that were far nicer than anything we could afford at the time.

One time my wife and I were house-sitting for an owner who had a Porsche in his garage. Before he left, he told me I could park my beat-up, battered Grand Prix on the street and drive his Porsche instead. He didn't have to tell me twice! I drove that car to school and back every day, and I took the scenic route in both directions.

When I got home, however, my wife made it a point to say, "That's not your car, Tony." In fact, she reminded me that nothing in the house belonged to us. We were simply managing what other people had worked for and built over time. That's the foundational principle at the heart of the concept we call stewardship.

What ideas or images come to mind when you hear the word *stewardship?*

When have you been assigned to manage resources that belonged to another person? What happened?

This week we've explored key components of living as individuals in the kingdom of God. We've seen that following God's kingdom agenda has a significant impact on our priorities as kingdom citizens, on our identity as disciples, and on our calling as followers of Christ.

Today we're going to explore the responsibility of kingdom citizens to serve as stewards in God's house. We'll focus on one of Jesus' parables from the Gospel of Luke.

Read Luke 19:11-27. What are your initial reactions to these verses?

What does this passage teach about stewardship and our role as stewards in God's kingdom?

# GOD OWNS IT ALL

Look at the way Jesus began His parable:

> *A nobleman went to a distant country to receive a kingdom for himself, and then return. And he called ten of his slaves, and gave them ten minas and said to them, "Do business with this until I come back."*
> LUKE 19:12-13

Right away you have to appreciate Jesus' efficiency as a storyteller, because He packed quite a bit of symbolism and prophecy into those two sentences. Basically, Jesus was referring to Himself as the nobleman, and He was predicting His departure from this world to lay claim to the kingdom He planned to rule by virtue of His victory on Calvary. "Distant country" (v. 12) meant heaven, from which Jesus would return one day to reestablish His visible kingdom on earth.

In the meantime Jesus made it clear that He's given us resources to manage for Him while He's away, and He expects us to manage them well until He returns.

What are some of the primary resources you're currently managing as a member of God's kingdom?

One of the most important truths revealed by this parable is that God owns everything in this world, not to mention everything in the universe and any other pockets of creation we haven't discovered. Everything belongs to God because He created everything.

Notice that the slaves in Jesus' parable made no financial contributions of their own. They were able to work with only what they'd been given. It's the same with us. We come into this world with nothing, and we take nothing with us when we leave. While on earth, we're simply stewards of what God chooses to give us.

> Read the following passages of Scripture and record what they teach about God's ownership of all things.
>
> Job 38:1-11
>
> Psalm 50:10-15
>
> 1 Corinthians 6:19-20

God owns everything, and He doesn't share ownership with anyone but Himself—because He's God. You and I will do well to remember that fact as we attempt to live out God's kingdom agenda in a culture that shouts, "Mine!" more loudly and ferociously than a toddler guarding a candy dish.

## WE'RE RESPONSIBLE

Just because we as human beings don't truly *own* anything in this world doesn't mean we don't *have* anything. Obviously, we have an abundance of possessions and resources at our disposal; in fact, many of us have an overabundance. But we serve as stewards of those resources and possessions, not owners. That means we have a responsibility to manage what we've been given in a way that will please and benefit the Owner.

In Jesus' parable the nobleman's command gets to the heart of our responsibility as stewards: "Do business with this until I come back" (Luke 19:13). Because we're members of God's kingdom, our business involves advancing God's kingdom and glorifying Him by carrying out His kingdom agenda.

In other words, we as stewards in God's kingdom are responsible to use the resources we've been given to invest in God's kingdom agenda, not indulge our own desires.

> What's your response to the previous statement?

In what ways are you currently using the resources you've been given to invest in God's kingdom agenda?

Many Christians have trouble performing their role as stewards because they don't believe the Owner is going to come back one day and evaluate what they did with the time, talents, money, and possessions He gave them. They live as if this life on earth is the only life that matters.

The truth is that God will evaluate all Christians on our role as stewards in His kingdom. In verse 15 of Jesus' parable, the nobleman gathered all of the slaves to him after his return "so that he might know what business they had done." That's a sobering reality. You and I will both be judged on the business we've done with the resources we've been given.

Look again at Luke 19:15-26 in Jesus' parable. What emotions do you experience when you read these verses? Why?

Read 1 Corinthians 3:10-15. What do these verses teach about our role as stewards?

Paul said if our lives are to have eternal significance, we must build on the foundation of Jesus Christ. When we invest in the kingdom of God, we have an amazing opportunity to be part of something that lasts forever. To live as a steward in God's kingdom is to invest our time, talents, and other resources in ways that will pay dividends throughout eternity.

What steps can you take to raise your investment in God's kingdom?

I look forward with great anticipation to the day when I hear these words from the mouth of Jesus, my Lord: "Well done, good and faithful slave" (Matt. 25:21). If you want to hear those words as well, commit to investing the resources God has given you in advancing His kingdom agenda.

Week 3

# ONE FAMILY
# UNDER GOD

# START

**Welcome back to this small-group discussion of Kingdom Agenda.**

The previous session's application challenge encouraged you to contemplate your calling and purpose as you went about your everyday life. If you're comfortable, use the following questions to process that experience as a group.

- Describe a recent time when you felt your passions engaged by a specific ideal or cause.

- Describe a recent time when you felt that you were actively fulfilling or participating in your calling.

Describe what you liked best in the material from week 2. What questions do you have?

What does it look like to seek first God and His kingdom on a daily basis (see Matt. 6:33)?

What emotions do you experience when you hear the word *family?* Why?

To prepare for the DVD segment, read aloud the following verses.

> *The LORD God caused a deep sleep to fall upon the man, and he slept; then He took one*
> *of his ribs and closed up the flesh at that place. The LORD God fashioned into a woman*
> *the rib which He had taken from the man, and brought her to the man. The man said,*
> *"This is now bone of my bones,*
> *And flesh of my flesh;*
> *She shall be called Woman,*
> *Because she was taken out of Man."*
> *For this reason a man shall leave his father and his mother, and*
> *be joined to his wife; and they shall become one flesh. And the man*
> *and his wife were both naked and were not ashamed.*
> GENESIS 2:21-25

# WATCH

**Complete the viewer guide below as you watch DVD session 3.**

Nothing is more important to God's kingdom agenda than saving, preserving, and properly defining the _____.

The key to the definition of the family is to understand that the family was created for the _____.

God created the family to mirror His image as they exercise _____—rulership—on His behalf.

God gave each part of the family their roles so that they would be _____ under His rule.

Satan wants to remove dominion by messing up _____ so that the family is destroyed.

Your _____ trumps your sexuality.

Elohim refers to God's _____ (see Gen. 1). LORD (Jehovah) refers to God's _____ control or management (see Gen. 2).

God said He is not only the God of power but also the God of _____.

Whoever owns the family owns the _____.

At the heart of the definition of the expansion of the kingdom of God is the stability of the _____.

Satan gets _____ out of alignment with God, _____ out of alignment with their husbands and therefore out of alignment with God.

If we are going to save our nation, we'd better save our _____.

# RESPOND

*Use the following questions to discuss the DVD segment with your group.*

What did you appreciate most in Dr. Evans's teaching? Why?

What words describe your past experiences with family? Your current experiences?

Respond to Dr. Evans's statement: "The family was not first and foremost created for your happiness. That's a by-product and a benefit, not the reason that the family was created. The family was created for the kingdom."

How do families benefit and contribute to the world?

How do families benefit and contribute to God's kingdom?

What obstacles typically prevent or hinder families from being fully aligned with God's kingdom agenda?

How can we actively work to overcome and move away from those obstacles?

**Application.** As you think about your family this week, identify one or two foundational principles on which you'd like your family to operate—one or two principles that identify what's most important to your family's everyday life. Record those principles below.

1.

2.

**This week's Scripture memory.**

> *God said, "Let Us make man in Our image, according to Our likeness; and let them rule over the fish of the sea and over the birds of the sky and over the cattle and over all the earth, and over every creeping thing that creeps on the earth."*
> GENESIS 1:26

**Assignment.** Read week 3 and complete the activities before the next group experience.

## BUILDING YOUR HOUSE

During the Sermon on the Mount, Jesus' greatest teaching on His kingdom, He told the story of two men attempting to build two separate houses. Here's what happened next:

> *Everyone who hears these words of Mine and acts on them, may be compared to a wise man who built his house on the rock. And the rain fell, and the floods came, and the winds blew and slammed against that house; and yet it did not fall, for it had been founded on the rock. Everyone who hears these words of Mine and does not act on them, will be like a foolish man who built his house on the sand. The rain fell, and the floods came, and the winds blew and slammed against that house; and it fell—and great was its fall.*
> MATTHEW 7:24-27

Notice that the construction methods of these two men were almost identical. They used the same materials. They took the same amount of time to build. They faced the same rain, floods, and wind.

The only difference was the foundation on which each man chose to build. The foolish man wanted a lakefront villa, so he built his house on the sand. But the wise man did his construction on the rock.

Jesus' picture of building a house can represent a number of different things—an individual's life, a church, an organization, or even an entire society. But building a house can also refer quite literally to building a family unit in a home.

That's our focus for this week. If we seek to build our families on anything other than the rock of God's kingdom agenda, then our houses won't stand when life's trials and challenges come on us. Like every area of the Christian life, our families must be built on the stable, foundational kingdom principles expressed in God's Word.

*Day 1*

# THE FOUNDATIONS OF A KINGDOM FAMILY

If you've ever been house shopping, chances are good that you've found at least one property that was too good to be true. You know what I'm talking about, right? The house looked nice on the outside, had a big yard with a fence, and had the number of bedrooms you were looking for, plus a rec room in the basement—and the price was a lot lower than you expected.

Here's something I've learned from decades of being a homeowner and a property manager: if something looks too good to be true, it almost certainly is. Especially in real estate.

> When have you recently discovered something that was too good
> to be true? What happened?

There are a lot of physical houses in America today that look nice on the outside but have major problems hidden on the inside. Termites. Mold. Wood rot. A leaky roof. A leaky basement. Bad wiring. Corrosion in the pipes. I could go on and on.

In a similar way, there are a lot of families in today's culture that seem to have it all together. Yet if you take a look below the surface, you'll find that many families are dealing with several serious cracks in the foundation of their homes. I'm talking about divorce. Fatherlessness. Abuse. Neglect. Debt. Stress. Rebellion. Again, I could go on and on.

> How has our culture been affected by the previous issues?

> How have you been personally affected by cracks in the foundation
> of your family?

The disintegration of the family is the single most devastating issue facing our culture in general and our communities in particular. Why? Because families touch every area of society in a major way. To a large degree, the strengths and weaknesses of our families determine the strengths and weaknesses of our churches, our neighborhoods, our cities, our states, and even our nation as a whole.

Therefore, for our culture to experience moral, social, and spiritual renewal, we must begin by rebuilding the foundations of our families. There's no other way.

What's your response to the previous statements?

To begin working toward solutions in our homes, we need to understand the biblical foundations for families in the kingdom of God.

## THE PURPOSE OF THE FAMILY

An important principle of Bible study is called the law of first mention, which states that the first time a subject is mentioned in God's Word serves as an important baseline for interpreting teachings on that subject throughout the rest of God's Word. In other words, if you want to know what God thinks about something, look for the first time He mentioned it in His Word. Every additional mention of that topic will build on the first.

Not surprisingly, the concept of family is first mentioned in the Book of Genesis. Even before there was sin, there was family. In fact, the divine institution of family was originally established in a sinless environment created by God:

> God said, "Let Us make man in Our image, according to Our likeness; and let them rule over the fish of the sea and over the birds of the sky and over the cattle and over all the earth, and over every creeping thing that creeps on the earth." God created man in His own image, in the image of God He created him; male and female He created them.
> GENESIS 1:26-27

What do these verses teach about family?

Notice that word *Us* in verse 26, referring to the triune God who is Father, Son, and Holy Spirit. Also notice that we as human beings were created to bear this trinitarian image of God: "Let Us make man in Our image, according to Our likeness" (v. 26). An image is simply a mirror or a reflection of something else. So God created humanity—body, soul, and spirit—to mirror Him. Then He established humanity in the divine institution called family in order to reproduce His image.

Therefore, the goal of people in general—and the family in particular—is to serve as a mirror of God in the visible world. Simply put, the mission of the family is to replicate the image of God in history and to participate in His kingdom agenda on earth.

> How do your experiences with family compare to God's mission for families as described?

Here's a hard truth: being happy isn't the reason God created families. Helping people be happy isn't the mission for families here on earth. Yes, happiness in the home is a good thing, and it flows from God's primary goal for creating families. But the primary mission for every family in this world is nothing less than reflecting God's image through the advancement of His kingdom. Happiness is a side effect of that mission.

I stress that point because so many people today have made happiness their main goal in life. So many people value happiness to the point that if they're not experiencing that side effect—if they don't feel happy in their marriage or if they aren't happy in their role as a parent—they quit and move on. This is a major problem in today's culture, and it's caused by misunderstanding God's mission for families.

> Where do you see evidence in today's culture of people prioritizing happiness over God's mission for the family?

> How do you and your family members reflect the image of God in your everyday lives?

God established families to provide the opportunity and the framework for individuals to collectively carry out His kingdom agenda in history. And a major component of that agenda involves our dominion on earth.

## THE DOMINION OF THE FAMILY

Looking back at Genesis 1:26, we see that God had a specific role for people to carry out within the boundaries of His creation: "Let them rule." He reiterated that commission more completely in verse 28:

> *God blessed them; and God said to them, "Be fruitful and multiply, and fill the earth, and subdue it; and rule over the fish of the sea and over the birds of the sky and over every living thing that moves on the earth."*
> GENESIS 1:28

In this commission God delegated to humanity the full responsibility for managing His earthly creation. He chose to indirectly control the affairs of earth by allowing human beings, His image bearers, to exercise dominion. Therefore, all of us as individuals are agents on earth who serve as God's representatives to carry out His purposes in history.

Every person on earth doesn't carry dominion and responsibility for the *whole* earth; that would produce chaos. Rather, each of us is responsible to rule over the small spheres of geography and society in which we've been given influence. That's why families are so important to the process.

What are the main spheres of influence in which you operate each day?

What does it mean for you to rule in these spheres of influence as an agent of God's kingdom agenda?

There are several reasons the family is the central unit through which we as human beings carry out our dominion over the earth.

## 1. THE FAMILY IS THE VEHICLE THROUGH WHICH WE REPLICATE NEW BEARERS OF GOD'S IMAGE. As the family

multiplies, new children are commissioned, as we are, to "fill the earth, and subdue it" (v. 28). The family is also the primary way we train our children in what it means to carry the image of God and to rule the earth on His behalf.

## 2. FAMILY UNITS ALLOW US TO POOL RESOURCES AND FUNCTION AS A TEAM. They offer the emotional, financial, and practical support we need to carry out our work as God's agents in creation: "A cord of three strands is not quickly torn apart" (Eccl. 4:12).

How has your family strengthened your efforts to faithfully follow God's kingdom agenda?

What are some specific ways you and your family work together to advance the kingdom in your areas of dominion?

## 3. THE FAMILY'S COLLECTIVE DOMINION OVER THE EARTH IS A BLESSING. Genesis 1:28 says, "God blessed them; and God said to them, 'Be fruitful and multiply.' " When God established the family in the garden of Eden through Adam and Eve, He blessed them. He told them to be fruitful and multiply, thus enabling them to extend His blessing throughout the land and to those who came after them. This was a positive thing—a wonderful thing.

God blessed Adam and Eve by providing them with everything they needed to carry out His instructions and rule the earth on His behalf. He provided for them, and He provides for us as we seek to exercise dominion over the gardens we've been given.

How have you experienced God's provision in your efforts to manage your family and your other spheres of life?

Families are critical agents not only in our communities and our culture but also in God's kingdom agenda. And as we'll see tomorrow, God has used families to play a vital role in carrying out His agenda in history.

# THE FAMILY AS GOD'S INSTRUMENT

I once heard about a boy who lost one of his contact lenses. This was decades ago when contacts weren't disposable, so the boy spent a significant amount of time trying to find it because a replacement would be expensive. He got down on his hands and knees and crawled around the room for several minutes, squinting at the floor. Eventually he gave up and told his mother what had happened.

To his surprise, the boy's mother got down on her hands and knees and began to search. He was about to tell her it was hopeless—that he'd already looked the whole room over, and the lens was impossible to find—when she stood up and said, "Here it is."

The son was dumbfounded. He asked, "How did you find the contact lens in two minutes when I spent almost half an hour searching without finding anything?"

His mother said, "That's easy. You didn't find it because you were looking for a contact lens. I found it because I was looking for $250."

You see, sometimes our perspective can drastically change our perceived value of things.

> What are some possessions that you value more than anyone else in the world values them?

> What are some possessions that are prized as highly valuable by our culture but not by you?

I believe families are critically undervalued in today's culture. And one of the main reasons is that we have such a familiar perspective on the family as an institution. We're born into families. We're intimately familiar with our families from the moment we take our first breath, and many of us see and interact with our family members several times each day.

For that reason I'd like to help you gain a new perspective on the concept of family by exploring the different ways God has specifically used families to accomplish His kingdom agenda throughout history.

## FAMILY IN THE OLD TESTAMENT

It's clear throughout the Old Testament that when God wanted to initiate or accomplish something big in the world, He used families to get it done. For example, we've already seen that God entrusted the dominion of the entire world to Adam and Eve in the context of their new family.

In the same way, when the entire world had become corrupted by sin and God saw that "the wickedness of man was great on the earth" (Gen. 6:5), He chose to re-create and restore human civilization not just through Noah but through Noah's family:

> *Behold, I, even I am bringing the flood of water upon the earth, to destroy all flesh in which is the breath of life, from under heaven; everything that is on the earth shall perish. But I will establish My covenant with you; and you shall enter the ark—you and your sons and your wife, and your sons' wives with you.*
> GENESIS 6:17-18

In a way, Noah and his family served as a sequel to the story of Adam and Eve. They were "Adam and Eve 2.0," but this time God worked through an extended family rather than just a husband and a wife.

Read Genesis 8:13-22. What are the similarities between God's charge to Noah's family and His original charge to Adam and Eve in Genesis 1:26-30?

What are the differences between those two charges?

Centuries later, when God wanted to raise up a people who were set apart for Him, He once again used the divine institution of family to initiate His work. This time He chose Abraham (also called Abram) and Sarah to be His instruments:

*The LORD said to Abram,*
*"Go forth from your country,*
*And from your relatives*
*And from your father's house,*
*To the land which I will show you;*
*And I will make you a great nation,*
*And I will bless you,*
*And make your name great;*
*And so you shall be a blessing;*
*And I will bless those who bless you,*
*And the one who curses you I will curse.*
*And in you all the families of the earth will be blessed."*
GENESIS 12:1-3

Notice the end of verse 3: "In you all the families of the earth will be blessed." God not only worked through a single family in His plan to bless the world, but He also intentionally planned for His blessing to spread to all families. God loves to work through and for the families in His kingdom.

How have you been blessed by your family?

How has your family been blessed through God's plan for Abraham and his family?

Also notice that God specifically and intentionally used the dynamics of family life to spread His message and His blessing throughout the world. It wasn't just that God wanted to work through Abraham, who happened to be in a family. No, God placed Abraham in the context of a family so that this man could do the work of God's kingdom agenda:

> *The LORD said, "Shall I hide from Abraham what I am about to do, since Abraham will surely become a great and mighty nation, and in him all the nations of the earth will be blessed? For I have chosen him, **so that he may command his children and his household after him to keep the way of the LORD by doing righteousness and justice,** so that the LORD may bring upon Abraham what He has spoken about him."*
> GENESIS 18:17-19, emphasis added

Do you see the progression? God's promises to bless Abraham and build a nation were directly connected to Abraham's influence on his children. God instructed Abraham to train his children, along with his entire household, to live their lives under God's plan.

In other words, Abraham's greatness as the father of a nation was tied to his performance as a father to his children.

How have you and your family extended God's blessing in your neighborhood, church, and other spheres of life?

## FAMILY IN THE NEW TESTAMENT

God was also intentional in the New Testament about using the institution of family to carry out His agenda. It's significant that when God chose to redeem the entire world through the incarnation and eventual sacrifice of His Son, He did so by placing Jesus in the context of a family on earth:

> *Joseph also went up from Galilee, from the city of Nazareth, to Judea, to the city of David which is called Bethlehem, because he was of the house and family of David, in order to register along with Mary, who was engaged to him, and was with child.*
> LUKE 2:4-5

Why is it important that Jesus' earthly father "was of the house and family of David" (v. 4)?

The members of Jesus' earthly family were descendants of kings. This lineage gave Jesus the legal right to the throne of His ancestor David. At the same time, Jesus' earthly family was a normal household that functioned as most households have functioned for thousands of years. It was within that household, within that normal family, that Jesus thrived:

> *He went down with [His parents] and came to Nazareth, and He continued in subjection to them; and His mother treasured all these things in her heart. And Jesus kept increasing in wisdom and stature, and in favor with God and men.*
> LUKE 2:51-52

Finally, it's interesting to note that the New Testament authors used family imagery when they communicated about the church and God's kingdom plan for this world. They consistently used terms such as *brothers, sisters, household,* and so on to describe members of God's kingdom.

Read the following passages of Scripture and record ways they use family imagery to describe God's kingdom and work.

John 14:1-3

1 Timothy 3:14-15

Revelation 19:7-10

Families are vital, honored tools in God's kingdom—tools He regularly uses to accomplish His kingdom agenda here on earth. Throughout the rest of this week, we'll explore the importance of aligning yourself as a member of a family under God's rule and within the particular context of your family role.

# KINGDOM HUSBANDS

Once when I took my car to the dealership for a checkup, the mechanic told me that the tires on my car weren't wearing evenly; they'd been worn down in such a way that one side of the tires contained more tread than the other side. This was a problem because it had the potential to make my driving experience unstable.

My first thought was that I needed new tires, but the mechanic corrected me: "The tires are just a symptom of the problem," he told me. "The root issue is that your car is out of alignment. You need to fix that first, or you'll just end up with more uneven wear on your new tires."

When I look around at marriages and families in today's culture, I see a lot of wear and tear. I see a lot of people who are worn down and a lot of relationships that need help.

> When have you recently noticed or heard about people feeling worn down in their marriages?

> In what ways have you seen the institution of marriage become worn down in today's culture?

So how do we resolve this social crisis? How do we fix the dysfunction and deterioration occurring in our marriages—even in the institution of marriage? We do so by returning to and honoring the principle of alignment God has given us in His Word.

## ALIGNMENT IN GOD'S KINGDOM

One thing we need to understand about God is that He typically uses a chain of command when He operates in history. Obviously, God is at the top of that chain, but He often chooses to exercise His authority in this world through people.

For example, we've already seen that God made Adam and Eve stewards in the garden of Eden. They were given dominion over the whole earth; they were commanded to rule over the created world. But God was still in charge. In the same way, God anointed David to be the king over Israel and to rule over God's people. But David's authority as the king was still subject to God's authority as Creator.

These are illustrations of the principle of alignment. God has designed a hierarchy in which we, as members of His kingdom, come under His authority as we rule and lead in our different spheres of life. When we're properly aligned according to this hierarchy, we experience the blessings of God's kingdom. When we try to be autonomous—when we seek to break away from God's chain of command, as Satan did (see Luke 10:18)—we experience all kinds of problems.

> When have you attempted to break away from alignment with God? What happened?

Here's how the principle of alignment applies to the institution of marriage:

> *I want you to understand that Christ is the head of every man, and*
> *the man is the head of a woman, and God is the head of Christ.*
> 1 CORINTHIANS 11:3

> What's your initial reaction to this verse? Why?

The chain of command here is clear: God, Christ, man, and woman. Therefore, the first and most important job of every kingdom husband is to recognize that he's under the authority of Jesus Christ. Yes, husbands are called to lead and demonstrate authority in their homes—but only when that authority is validated by submission to Christ.

When a husband refuses the authority of Christ and attempts to follow his own way, he forfeits any expectation of submission from his wife. After all, for a wife to align herself under a rebellious husband would be to participate in his rebellion, causing more damage to the family. The husband's submission to Christ is vital.

## THREE KEYS FOR HUSBANDS

It's time to get practical. We know from Ephesians 5 that husbands are called to "love [their] wives, just as Christ also loved the church and gave Himself up for her" (v. 25). But what does that mean? Obviously, there's an element of sacrifice; a husband should give himself up for his wife. But what does that look like in real life?

Let's look at 1 Peter 3:7 to get some answers. This verse highlights three specific, practical ways for husbands to love their wives according to God's Word:

> *You husbands in the same way, live with your wives in an understanding*
> *way, as with someone weaker, since she is a woman; and show her honor as a*
> *fellow heir of the grace of life, so that your prayers will not be hindered.*
> 1 PETER 3:7

What emotions do you experience when you read this verse? Why?

## 1. LIVE WITH YOUR WIFE. The first thing we see is that husbands are to "live with [their] wives in an understanding way." I know some husbands will read this and think, *That's easy. We're in the same house, so I have to live with her.*

Not so fast. To live with your wife is to be a functioning, fully committed member of your home. Too many husbands believe their role entitles them to work eight hours at their jobs and then come home to rest. They feel it's the wife's job to take care of the house and everything in it, even if the wife has her own job outside the home.

Where do you see this mindset reflected in today's culture?

A kingdom husband is called to live *with* his wife. He's called to be understanding. He's called to be a teammate. He's called to be a partner in the home. In fact, obeying God's Word in this area means that when a husband goes home, he arrives at his second job.

How does your family measure up to this standard from God's Word?

## 2. HONOR YOUR WIFE. Kingdom husbands are also called to honor their wives: "Show her honor" (1 Pet. 3:7). This means a husband places his wife in a position of significance and treats her as someone special—someone worthy of being cherished.

I often ask husbands, "When was your last date with your wife?" I'm not talking about coming home and saying, "What do you want to do tonight?" That's just lazy.

No, a date is when a husband says, "Honey, I've got this evening all planned out. I've been thinking about you all day, and I'd like to take you out and show you how much you mean to me." That kind of experience communicates honor and value to a wife.

What makes you feel honored and cherished by your spouse?

What steps have you recently taken to honor and cherish your spouse?

**3. PRAY WITH YOUR WIFE.** The last and most important way a kingdom man becomes a real kingdom husband is by intentionally praying with his wife. Peter commanded husbands to live with their wives and honor their wives "so that your prayers will not be hindered" (1 Pet. 3:7).

Please hear me: if there's no spiritual dynamic in the relationship between husband and wife, there won't be *anything* dynamic after a few years. If a husband and a wife don't have a heavenly foundation, they'll end up with a hellish relationship.

Peter said a man's wife is his "fellow heir of the grace of life" (1 Pet. 3:7). From the very beginning, God's design was for a husband and a wife to come together to form "one flesh" (Gen. 2:24). Therefore, husbands and wives no longer relate to God solely as individuals. He views them as one flesh, one being. So it's critically important for them to approach God together and to be on the same page spiritually.

What steps can you take to improve your prayer life with your spouse?

To live as a kingdom husband under the authority of Jesus Christ looks much different from the way husbands typically operate in today's culture. Kingdom husbands live with their wives, honor their wives, and pray with their wives in obedience to God's Word.

# KINGDOM WIVES

This week we're exploring the impact of following God's kingdom agenda as families. We've already looked at the foundations necessary for building a kingdom family, and we've seen ways God specifically used families to accomplish His will throughout history.

Yesterday we examined the implications of God's kingdom agenda for husbands. Today we'll explore what it means to be a kingdom wife.

How would you summarize what it means to be a good husband?

How would you summarize what it means to be a good wife?

We'll start today's discussion by highlighting a concept you may find distasteful.

## THE TRUTH ABOUT SUBMISSION

There's no getting around the fact that *submit* and *submission* are increasingly unpopular words in today's culture. In almost every case our society views a decision to submit as an act of weakness—as something to be avoided at all costs.

What ideas or images come to mind when you hear the word *submit?*

What emotions do you typically experience when you submit to someone or something? Why?

The reason we need to explore the concept of submission is that God, through His Word, calls wives in His kingdom to submit to their earthly husbands. We saw that yesterday in 1 Corinthians 11:3: "Christ is the head of every man, and the man is the head of a woman."

In God's hierarchy every husband is called to submit to Christ as an act of obedience, and every wife is called to submit to her husband in the same spirit of obedience. That's what the apostle Paul wanted to make clear when he wrote these words:

> *Wives, submit to your own husbands as to the Lord, for the husband is the head of the wife as Christ is the head of the church. He is the Savior of the body. Now as the church submits to Christ, so wives are to submit to their husbands in everything.*
> EPHESIANS 5:22-24

What's your initial reaction to these verses?

Let's make sure we understand what this Scripture is saying. The Greek word translated *submit* is *hupotasso,* which means *to voluntarily place oneself under the authority of another.* That's an important concept. Biblical submission is first and foremost voluntary; it's never forced or coerced.

Rather, biblical submission involves a willingness to submit yourself to the authority of another. For a husband, that means submitting to God. For a wife, that means submitting both to God and to her husband. This is the alignment God designed for families, and problems arise when either partner chooses to operate outside his or her given role.

How does your family measure up to this standard from God's Word?

I want to clarify two truths about biblical submission before we move on.

## 1. BIBLICAL SUBMISSION DOESN'T MEAN A WIFE FORFEITS THE RIGHT TO HAVE OPINIONS, MAKE DECISIONS, OR DISAGREE WITH HER HUSBAND. As we saw yesterday, husbands are called to live with their wives in a way that emphasizes teamwork and mutual respect. A family should never degenerate into a dictatorship.

Rather, biblical submission is primarily a partnership. A kingdom wife is responsible to be involved and informed in every area of the household. She should work with her husband to guide the direction of the family, and she should correct or confront her husband when she feels that he's out of alignment with Christ. At the same time, she should align herself underneath her husband and defer to his authority when it's time for a final decision.

Of course, a wife shouldn't willingly submit to or follow her husband into rebellion against God. A husband's headship in the family is valid only as long as he operates within the divine mandates, commands, and principles of God's Word.

Who among your friends and family would you characterize as a good example of a kingdom wife?

## 2. BIBLICAL SUBMISSION DOESN'T MEAN A DIFFERENCE IN VALUE BETWEEN HUSBANDS AND WIVES. In other words, when a kingdom wife aligns herself underneath her kingdom husband, she doesn't become less valuable as a child of God or less important in her family. The principle of alignment speaks to the way husbands and wives function in their families. It's not a measure of value.

People have been confused about this point throughout history because the Bible often describes wives in terms of helping or complementing their husbands. Look at Genesis 2:18, for example:

> *The LORD God said, "It is not good for the man to be alone;*
> *I will make him a helper suitable for him."*
> GENESIS 2:18

It's enlightening to realize that the Hebrew word translated *helper* in Genesis 2 is used several other times throughout the Old Testament to describe God Himself. For example, Psalm 33:20 says:

> *Our soul awaits for the LORD;*
> *He is our **help** and our shield."*
> PSALM 33:20, emphasis added

The same word used of God is also used to describe wives as helpers of their husbands.

Read the following passages of Scripture and record what they teach about God's serving as helper.

Deuteronomy 33:26

Psalm 70:5

To be a helper in God's kingdom is to provide strength and completion. It's not a demeaning designation but an overwhelmingly positive term.

## TRUSTING GOD

I understand that it's often difficult for women to accept the principle of alignment and the concept of biblical submission, especially in today's culture. Let's be frank: there's no such thing as a perfect husband who's perfectly aligned with the will of Christ. Therefore, to submit can feel that you're taking a risk.

In addition, God calls a wife to respect and submit to her husband even when they have a difference of opinion and even when her husband isn't worthy of respect and submission. That's scary. It can be difficult to trust that way.

What emotions do you experience when you think of practicing biblical submission in your family? Why?

In the end, however, biblical submission isn't about a wife trusting her husband. It's about trusting God. It's about a wife functionally aligning herself under her husband's authority in order to obediently align herself with the role God has assigned her as part of His kingdom agenda.

Read 1 Peter 3:1-6. How do these verses contribute to your understanding of biblical submission?

According to Peter, what are the benefits of biblical submission?

Don't let fear keep you from experiencing God's best for your relationships. Trust Him. Surrender to Him. Be faithful and patient as you seek to live out His kingdom agenda in your life, your family, and your marriage.

*Day 5*

# KINGDOM PARENTS

I once heard about a man who traveled the country giving speeches. His favorite lecture was called "The Ten Commandments for Parenting." He wrote it based on his experiences raising his young child, and he gave that lecture wherever he could find people to listen.

Then he and his wife had a second child. He still traveled the country whenever he could find the time, and he still gave his favorite lecture. But the people who'd heard him before noticed that he'd changed the title of the lecture to "The Ten Suggestions for Parents."

When the man and his wife had their third child, he stopped lecturing altogether. By then he'd figured out that it's much easier to talk about parenting than to roll up your sleeves and actually do what parents need to do.

What's the best advice you've received about being a parent?

What are the biggest challenges you currently face as a parent?

The primary job of kingdom parents is to raise kingdom kids in such a way that they become kingdom adults. That's not an easy goal to accomplish, but that's our mission.

To get us moving in the right direction, let's explore four truths from the Bible that will help us align our role and responsibilities as parents with God's kingdom agenda.

## ENCOURAGE YOUR CHILDREN

Ephesians 6:4 is the primary text for today. All four of the truths we'll explore can be found in this one verse:

> *Fathers, do not provoke your children to anger, but bring them*
> *up in the discipline and instruction of the Lord.*
> EPHESIANS 6:4

What are your initial reactions to this verse? Why?

This verse is addressed to fathers because, on a theological level, God views the father as the representative head of the home, according to the principle of alignment. But on a practical level, the truths contained in these verses apply equally to fathers and mothers.

Paul began this passage by making a negative statement: "Do not provoke your children to anger." He did the same thing in Colossians 3:21: "Fathers, do not exasperate your children, so that they will not lose heart." Stated in a positive way, we as Christian parents are called to actively encourage our children, not discourage them. Our children need to know beyond a shadow of a doubt that we love them and support them.

How did your parents encourage and support you as a child?

What caused you to feel provoked or exasperated when growing up?

One of the best ways to encourage your children is to intentionally make them a high priority in your life. That means investing your time and other resources not just in their development as people but also in their dreams and passions. That also means when conflicts arise between investing in your kids and advancing your career or ministry, your kids should win most of the time.

On a scale of 1 to 10, how successful are you at intentionally making your children a priority?

| 1 | 2 | 3 | 4 | 5 | 6 | 7 | 8 | 9 | 10 |
|---|---|---|---|---|---|---|---|---|---|
| Not successful | | | | | | | | | Very successful |

Another way you can encourage your children is by blessing them. This is a powerful, biblical concept. In the ancient world the blessing was a key component of family life. It involved a father's transferring the family mantle and inheritance to his son. It was a way to publicly recognize and communicate a child's significance.

Read each passage and summarize the blessing communicated.

Genesis 27:26-29

Genesis 49:8-12

How have you been affected by blessings you've received from others?

The kind of blessing and encouragement I'm talking about is different from generic praise. If your child gets an A in school and you say, "Good job," that's generic praise. That's simply acknowledging an accomplishment. There's nothing wrong with praise, of course, but it has a tendency to disappear when your kids aren't doing what you want or expect.

Genuine encouragement isn't related to what your kids achieve; it's related to who they are. You bless your children when you tell them with no reservations and no restrictions that you love and support them and that you'll always love and support them simply because they're yours.

What can you do to bless your children this week?

## NURTURE YOUR CHILDREN

A second way we can fulfill our kingdom role as parents is to nurture our children. That's why Paul commanded us to "bring them up" in Ephesians 6:4.

That's an ambiguous phrase—"bring them up." But Paul used the same Greek word in Ephesians 5:29, and that verse gives us some context: "No one ever hated his own flesh, but *nourishes and cherishes* it, just as Christ also does the church" (emphasis added). So in the same way Christ nurtures and cares for the church, we're called to nurture and care for our children.

In what ways do you nurture and nourish your children?

At the end of Luke 2, we're told that Jesus was nurtured by His earthly family during His childhood. As a result, He "kept increasing in wisdom and stature, and in favor with God and men" (v. 52). In other words, Jesus grew intellectually, physically, spiritually, and socially as a member of His family.

Most parents today are on board with three of those dimensions. Our culture is desperate to see children grow physically, intellectually, and socially—and that's good. Children need to be nurtured in all of those areas. But we often leave out the spiritual part. Even in the church some parents feel that Bible-study teachers and youth ministers are responsible for helping their children develop spiritually.

Here's the truth: God didn't give your children to a school or a church to raise; He gave them to you. Kingdom parents are responsible for the physical, intellectual, social, and certainly the spiritual nourishment of their kids.

> How do you personally invest your time and resources in the spiritual nourishment of your children?

## DISCIPLINE YOUR CHILDREN

Getting back to Ephesians 6:4, we see that Paul called for Christian parents to "bring [children] up in the discipline ... of the Lord." In other words, we're biblically commanded to discipline our kids.

> How were you typically disciplined as a child?

> What methods do you use to discipline your children?

Correction is one component of biblical discipline. All human beings are born with a sin nature, which is why children don't need to be taught how to cheat, fight, or throw a temper tantrum; it's all ingrained. That's also why it's vital for us as parents to correct our kids. We're called to actively turn them away from sin—using punishment when necessary and appropriate—and toward God's kingdom values and Christlike character.

Many people don't understand that correction is an act of love. Hebrews 12:6 says:

> *Those whom the LORD loves He disciplines,*
> *And He scourges every son whom He receives.*
> HEBREWS 12:6

The corrective element of discipline is vital for children, but it should always be connected with love. God corrects us in love, and He calls us to do the same for our kids.

# INSTRUCT YOUR CHILDREN

There's also a second component of discipline: training. Just as we use punishment to move our children away from sinful patterns, we also actively teach and train our children how to live according to God's kingdom agenda. As Proverbs 22:6 says:

> *Train up a child in the way he should go,*
> *Even when he is old he will not depart from it.*
> PROVERBS 22:6

This truth is reflected in Ephesians 6:4, where Paul commands us to raise our kids not just in the discipline of the Lord but also in the "instruction of the Lord." In other words, Christian parents must intentionally teach their children about God and His ways. I love the way Moses described this principle:

> *These words, which I am commanding you today, shall be on your heart. You shall*
> *teach them diligently to your sons and shall talk of them when you sit in your house*
> *and when you walk by the way and when you lie down and when you rise up.*
> *You shall bind them as a sign on your hand and they shall be as frontals on your*
> *forehead. You shall write them on the doorposts of your house and on your gates.*
> DEUTERONOMY 6:6-9

Christian parent, God has commanded you to diligently teach your children about His kingdom and their place in His agenda. God has commanded you to teach your kids consistently: when you sit, when you stand, when you walk, when you get ready to sleep, and when you wake up. These verses make it clear that God has commanded you to teach your kids conspicuously, doing whatever it takes to instruct your kids about God.

On a scale of 1 to 10, how satisfied are you with the spiritual education of your children?

| 1 | 2 | 3 | 4 | 5 | 6 | 7 | 8 | 9 | 10 |
|---|---|---|---|---|---|---|---|---|----|
| Not satisfied | | | | | | | | | Very satisfied |

What steps can you take to be more diligent, consistent, and conspicuous in the ways you teach your children about God?

Whatever you do, don't give up. Don't throw in the towel as a spouse or a parent. Because you have a vital role to play, not only in your family but also in God's kingdom agenda.

Week 4

# ONE CHURCH
# UNDER GOD

# START

**Welcome back to this small-group discussion of Kingdom Agenda.**

The previous session's application challenge involved identifying one or two foundational principles for your family. What did you come up with? How would you describe the experience of contemplating and evaluating those principles?

Describe what you liked best in the material from week 3. What questions do you have?

What's your response to Dr. Evans's summary of the roles God has assigned to husbands and wives in families?

What ideas or images come to mind when you hear the word *church*? Why?

To prepare for the DVD segment, read aloud the following verses.

> *When Jesus came into the district of Caesarea Philippi, He was asking His disciples, "Who do people say that the Son of Man is?" And they said, "Some say John the Baptist; and others, Elijah; but still others, Jeremiah, or one of the prophets." He said to them, "But who do you say that I am?" Simon Peter answered, "You are the Christ, the Son of the living God." And Jesus said to him, "Blessed are you, Simon Barjona, because flesh and blood did not reveal this to you, but My Father who is in heaven. I also say to you that you are Peter, and upon this rock I will build My church; and the gates of Hades will not overpower it. I will give you the keys of the kingdom of heaven; and whatever you bind on earth shall have been bound in heaven, and whatever you loose on earth shall have been loosed in heaven."*
> MATTHEW 16:13-19

## WATCH

***Complete the viewer guide below as you watch DVD session 4.***

God has handed His people a Book called the _____, and all of the decisions made on the field of life are to be based on what's written in the Book.

The *ekklesia* in the Greek world was a legislative body that had _____ _____ to act on behalf of the general population.

The church is a legislative body that has the specific task of legislating on earth from _____.

The church is supposed to be an _____ agency, not a defensive agency.

Because we have watered down the meaning of church to be simply spiritual inspiration, we do not demonstrate the power and glory of the church's _____ in history.

Jesus wants to demonstrate, as the Head of the church, the _____ He has given His people to act on His behalf as His body in history.

The church does not exist for the church. The church exists for the _____.

We are to get the keys from the kingdom and use them on _____.

Binding and loosing mean _____ and _____. The two together mean authority.

The reason we're not experiencing more authority as God's people in history is that we're not using the authority designated from the _____.

It is incumbent now that the church takes the lead in impacting the _____.

## RESPOND

**Use the following questions to discuss the DVD segment with your group.**

What did you appreciate most in Dr. Evans's teaching? Why?

How have your experiences with local churches changed or evolved through the different phases of your life?

How would you summarize the relationship between local churches and the universal body of Christ we call the church?

Respond to Dr. Evans's definition of the church as "a legislative body that has the specific task of legislating on earth from heaven."

How have you seen churches benefit and contribute to their local communities?

What barriers often prevent churches from making a greater impact for God and His kingdom agenda?

What specific steps can we take as a group to widen our church's influence and impact in our community?

**Application.** Commit to pray this week for the churches in your local community. Pray daily for the church where you attend—that you and the other members will work together to advance God's kingdom agenda in your area. Also pray for the body that meets in every church building you pass as you drive around your community throughout the week.

**This week's Scripture memory.**

> *You also, as living stones, are being built up as a spiritual house for a holy*
> *priesthood, to offer up spiritual sacrifices acceptable to God through Jesus Christ.*
> 1 PETER 2:5

**Assignment.** Read week 4 and complete the activities before the next group experience.

## AN EMBASSY OF THE KINGDOM

Did you know you can find an American embassy in almost every recognized country on this planet? It's true. And the interesting thing about embassies is that they're sovereign territories, meaning they don't belong to the geographical country in which they're located. Rather, they belong to the countries from which they originate.

For example, if you walk into the American embassy in France, you're no longer in France. You're on American soil. Everyone within the borders of that embassy is bound by and must operate by the laws of America rather than the laws of France. The same is true for the American embassies in Spain, Chile, Japan, Australia, and so on.

In other words, every time you walk into an American embassy, you're walking into a little bit of America a long way from home.

In the same way, the church is supposed to be a little bit of heaven a long way from home. It's supposed to be the place where the laws and values of eternity operate in history. The church is supposed to be the place where weary people can go to find truth, acceptance, equality, freedom, safety, forgiveness, justice, and hope.

Unfortunately, what we see in society today is that the number of churches keeps increasing while the influence of the church continues to wane. We have more preaching, praising, and programs than we can handle, yet little spiritual power is demonstrated to the world. How can this be so?

The answer is that many elements of the church today bear little resemblance to the kingdom from which they came. In other words, the church has a limited impact on contemporary society because we as individuals and congregations have failed to function primarily from a kingdom perspective.

This week we'll go back to the drawing board and examine basic biblical components of what it means to be a church that's properly aligned with God's kingdom agenda.

*Day 1*

# UNDERSTANDING THE CHURCH

Today marks the halfway point of our study on God's kingdom agenda. That makes this a great place for us to review the major themes we've covered so far.

What are the main things you've learned about the kingdom in this study?

How has this study positively affected your recent actions and attitudes?

God's kingdom has been the starting point for this study. Because God created the universe, His kingdom technically has no boundaries; He's the rightful Ruler of all things because He's the Creator of all things. On a functional level, however, we've defined God's kingdom as the realm in which He chooses to exercise His divine authority.

God's kingdom is larger than the temporal, political, and social realms in which we live as human beings, and it isn't confined to what we label as Christian in this world. God's kingdom is both happening now (see Mark 1:15) and still to come (see Matt. 16:28). It's near to us (see Luke 17:21) but also far away from us (see Matt. 7:21) because it originates in heaven. Most importantly, God's kingdom operates by the rule of God (theocracy) rather than the rule of man (homocracy).

That's why the psalmist wrote these powerful words:

> *The LORD has established his throne in heaven,*
> *and his kingdom rules over all.*
> PSALM 103:19, NIV

Once we understand the basics of God's kingdom, our next step is to begin unfolding the plan and program God is currently executing in His kingdom—His blueprint for creation. We've referred to that blueprint as God's kingdom agenda, and we've defined it as the visible manifestation of the comprehensive rule of God over every area of life.

This is where the rubber hits the road for us as human beings. Because God's kingdom doesn't originate in this world, He often uses specific agencies to carry out His kingdom agenda in this world. He works through individuals, families, churches, and nations to carry out His will. Therefore, we continually have the opportunity to align ourselves under God's kingdom agenda, which leads to life, or to rebel against God's kingdom agenda, which leads to chaos, confusion, and calamity.

We've already explored the implications of God's kingdom agenda for individuals and families. This week we'll focus on the church.

> What feelings or emotions do you experience when you think about the church? Why?

## LIVING STONES

Can you think of a definition of *church?* That's a tough question but also an important one. We're going to explore the purpose and mission of the church this week, but we won't get far without a solid understanding of what the church is.

> How would you explain the concept of the church to someone who isn't part of the church?

I'm going to provide my own definition of *church* at the end of today's material, but I want to get there by focusing on two key biblical images that help us understand what God intended the church to be.

The first comes from Jesus in Matthew 16:17-18. This is an important passage of Scripture because it's the first place the term *church* is mentioned in God's Word. Pay attention to Jesus' imagery in these verses, especially in terms of rocks and stones:

> *Jesus said to him, "Blessed are you, Simon Barjona, because flesh and blood did not reveal this to you, but My Father who is in heaven. I also say to you that you are Peter, and upon this rock I will build My church; and the gates of Hades will not overpower it."*
> MATTHEW 16:17-18

Get the whole context for Jesus' words by reading Matthew 16:13-20. What are your initial reactions to this passage?

What do these verses teach about the church?

After Peter's declaration that Jesus is the Messiah, Jesus responded by blessing Peter and giving him a new name. Jesus called him *petros,* the Greek word for a single stone of a size that can be thrown or carried. But when Jesus said, "Upon this rock I will build My church" (v. 18), He used the Greek word *petra,* which refers to a cliff or a large collection of rocks.

In other words, Jesus didn't say He'd build His church on Peter, an individual stone *(petros).* He said He'd build His church on a huge mass *(petra)* of stones like Peter—men and women who recognize Jesus as the Messiah—by joining those stones together into a single entity.

What does Jesus' vision for the church communicate about you as a church member?

Peter himself expressed this idea in his epistle to the early church:

> *You also, as living stones, are being built up as a spiritual house for a holy priesthood, to offer up spiritual sacrifices acceptable to God through Jesus Christ.*
> 1 PETER 2:5

The apostle Paul also used this imagery when he taught new believers what it means to be part of the church:

> *You are no longer strangers and aliens, but you are fellow citizens with the saints, and are of God's household, having been built on the foundation of the apostles and prophets, Christ Jesus Himself being the corner stone, in whom the whole building, being fitted together, is growing into a holy temple in the Lord, in whom you also are being built together into a dwelling of God in the Spirit.*
> EPHESIANS 2:19-22

So the church is a living collection of individual stones joined together to serve as the foundation of God's kingdom work in this world. Notice that the church doesn't exist solely in terms of stones that are living and breathing now; rather, we who live as Christians today are "fellow citizens with the saints" (v. 19). The church is the unified collection of *all* Christians throughout history.

Also notice that we aren't isolated from God in our attempts to be the church. Instead, we are "of God's household" (v. 19). Jesus Himself is the cornerstone of the church; we are constructed around Him. And we're being made "into a dwelling of God in the Spirit" (v. 22). In other words, the church is supported by all three members of the Trinity.

How has being a member of the church helped you experience and interact with God?

## THE BODY OF CHRIST

The second biblical image that helps us define and understand the church is the connection Paul made between it and a living, breathing body: the church is the body of Christ:

> *He gave some as apostles, and some as prophets, and some as evangelists, and some as pastors and teachers, for the equipping of the saints for the work of service, to the building up of the body of Christ; until we all attain to the unity of the faith.*
> EPHESIANS 4:11-13

How do these verses contribute to your understanding of the church?

I love the intimacy expressed in the idea of the church as "the body of Christ" (v. 12). God intended for us as individual Christians to be so connected, so unified that we operate like a human body. We're like muscles, organs, and tissues with different features and different functions, yet all work together for a single goal, and all are directed toward that goal by the same Head, who is Christ.

When do you feel most connected with other Christians around the world?

What steps can you take to interact with a wider and more diverse collection of fellow Christians?

Don't forget that this unity of purpose also applies to your local church. So far we've been talking about the universal church—the collection of all Christians throughout history. But we need to understand that the universal church also includes the local-church congregations in cities and communities around the world. Each of these congregations exists as an expression of the universal body of Christ.

What do you appreciate most about your local church? Why?

What unified kingdom purpose does your church communicate to the world?

In summary, the church is a collection of living stones, and the church is a body. The key concept in both of these images is a group of individual elements that join together to form something new—something both alive and unified.

With that in mind, here's how I define *church* in my Tony Evans Dictionary:

**CHURCH:** A COMMUNITY OF INDIVIDUALS SPIRITUALLY LINKED TOGETHER TO REFLECT AND LEGISLATE THE VALUES OF GOD'S KINGDOM

As you can see, it's hard to define the church without hinting at the church's purpose in this world. That's what we'll study tomorrow.

*Day 2*
# THE PURPOSE OF THE CHURCH

When people attempt to understand or explain a complicated idea, they typically use six journalistic questions as a framework for defining that idea. Those questions are: Who? What? When? Where? Why? How?

We're certainly exploring a complicated idea when it comes to the church, and yesterday we spent quite a bit of time examining the *what* question: What is the church? We ultimately answered that question with the following definition: the church is a community of individuals spiritually linked together to reflect and legislate the values of God's kingdom.

> How do your experiences as a member of the church compare to the previous definition? Explain.

By now you've probably noticed that our definition answers not only the *what* question but also the *why* question. The purpose of the church involves both reflecting and legislating the values of God's kingdom. Only by fulfilling that purpose can the church as a whole—not to mention individual congregations—become properly aligned with God's kingdom agenda.

With that in mind, let's gain a better understanding of the church's purpose and how that purpose connects with our lives in God's kingdom.

## REFLECTING GOD'S KINGDOM VALUES

If you've recently been to a movie theater, chances are good that you sat through several previews for upcoming movies. These movie trailers are designed to entice you as a moviegoer by showing you clips from the best parts of the movie—chase scenes, love scenes, fight scenes, and so on.

In other words, the singular goal of these previews is to whet your appetite for a movie that's not yet available so that you'll be more likely to buy a ticket once it's released.

> What elements in a movie preview (action, suspense, romance, etc.) typically motivate you to watch the entire movie?

It may sound strange, but one purpose of the church is similar to the purpose of those movie trailers. See, there's a big show coming to town. It's called the kingdom of God. Jesus Christ is the main star, and it will be a worldwide production. Until the kingdom is fully manifested on earth, however, God has left little previews throughout the world in order to whet people's appetites for the big show.

You and I are those previews, along with every other member of the universal church. We're called to reflect the values of God's kingdom in such a way that people outside the kingdom are enticed by it. They should see our lives and recognize that we're living according to a different, more appealing agenda.

The same idea is true for local churches. Each congregation in a city or community is supposed to serve as a visible representation of how God's kingdom will operate one day. This should happen when the members of a congregation gather together to worship God, learn about God, and support one another. It should also happen when those same church members disperse into the community and live as followers of Christ in a culture that needs to know about Christ.

> In what ways does your life reflect the values of God's kingdom
> in a positive way?

> In what ways does your local church reflect and promote the values
> of God's kingdom?

God designed the church to serve as an alternative model for the world about what life can and should be. When there's war in the world, there should be peace in the church (see Eph. 4:3). When there's oppression in the world, there should be liberation and justice in the church (see Jas. 2:1-9). When there are poverty and hunger in the world, there should be generosity and voluntary giving in the church. When there are racism, classism, and sexism in the world, there should be authentic oneness in the church (see Col. 3:11).

In other words, one purpose of the church is to reflect the values of God's kingdom in a way that's separate from the world yet still attractive to the world. That's our goal.

What obstacles prevent you as an individual from working more actively toward this goal?

How can those obstacles be overcome?

Jesus used a different image when He described our responsibility to reflect God's kingdom agenda as the church:

> *You are the light of the world. A city set on a hill cannot be hidden; nor does anyone light a lamp and put it under a basket, but on the lampstand, and it gives light to all who are in the house. Let your light shine before men in such a way that they may see your good works, and glorify your Father who is in heaven.*
> MATTHEW 5:14-16

When we reflect God's kingdom values in a world imprisoned by the corruption of sin, we'll stand out. We'll shine like the lights of a high city backlit against the night sky. And notice that we don't stand out so that the people of this world will think we're great or worth emulating. Rather, our commitment to reflect God's kingdom values will lead people to glorify our Father who is in heaven.

## LEGISLATING GOD'S KINGDOM VALUES

The second purpose of the church is to legislate the values of God's kingdom. By *legislate* I don't necessary mean that it's our function to create laws in society. Instead, I simply mean that the church is called to make things happen in God's kingdom. We're not just passive reflections of God's goodness; we also take an active role in carrying out God's kingdom agenda.

Look again at Matthew 16:18, where Jesus first used the word *church:*

> *I also say to you that you are Peter, and upon this rock I will build My church; and the gates of Hades will not overpower it.*
> MATTHEW 16:18

The Greek word translated *church* is *ekklesia.* In those days *ekklesia* was a term used to describe a group of people called out from the general population to serve in a government capacity. If you were part of an *ekklesia,* you were part of a governing body charged with making laws or guidelines for the benefit of your community.

This has interesting implications for what it means to be a church—an *ekklesia*—in today's world. When we say we're going to church or that we're members of a church, we're usually referring to a place where we passively encounter positive experiences. We go to church to find encouragement, to be taught, and to experience fellowship. Those are important aspects of church, but more should be involved.

Why do you go to church? What do you hope to encounter or experience?

To be part of the church as Jesus defined it is to be part of a spiritual legislative body tasked with enacting heaven's viewpoint in hell's society. In the midst of this world filled with sin, corruption, pain, and death, God has placed an *ekklesia*—a group of people called out to make a difference and improve the world through the execution of His kingdom agenda. That's the church.

Jesus Himself made it clear that we have power as members of the church:

> *I will give you the keys of the kingdom of heaven; and whatever*
> *you bind on earth shall have been bound in heaven, and whatever*
> *you loose on earth shall have been loosed in heaven.*
> MATTHEW 16:19

What's your initial reaction to this verse?

This verse is filled with legislative terms and imagery. The phrase "keys of the kingdom of heaven" refers to our access to God's heavenly authority. We've been given the opportunity to act on God's behalf to accomplish His agenda. Similarly, the references to *bind* and *loose* indicate that we as the church are called to take action when necessary.

In other words, from the first mention of the word *church,* Jesus made it clear that we're expected to both reflect God's values and work to enact His kingdom agenda in the world.

So what does that look like? What are we supposed to actually do as an *ekklesia* in our culture? Several passages of Scripture point us in the right direction.

Read the following passages of Scripture and record what they teach about making a difference in the world.

Micah 6:6-8

Romans 12:9-21

James 1:26-27

When have you recently had an opportunity to obey a command from one of the previous verses? What happened?

We as Christians today need to understand this: the job of the church isn't to adopt the values of the culture in which it resides or merely to analyze or assess that culture. Instead, the job of the church is to set heaven in the context of the culture so that people can see God at work in the midst of their everyday lives.

It's also the job of the church to advance God's kingdom by making disciples. Remember the Great Commission:

> *Go therefore and make disciples of all the nations, baptizing them in the name of the Father and the Son and the Holy Spirit, teaching them to observe all that I commanded you; and lo, I am with you always, even to the end of the age.*
> MATTHEW 28:19-20

The church has operated for too long on the defensive side of the battle. We've been content to react to the movements of hell rather than actively advancing the values of heaven and the breadth of God's kingdom.

If we could ever see God's kingdom as He sees it and if we could ever see one another as He sees us—individuals designed to come together in a unified goal under His overarching kingdom agenda—then the world would have to deal with the strength of the church of Jesus Christ. May that day come soon.

# UNITY IN THE CHURCH

If you've ever been the parent of a teenager, you know the experience can be frustrating. One main cause of this frustration is that teenagers often become hyperinterested in establishing their own individuality. They're in the process of figuring out who they are, which can lead to all kinds of crazy, rebellious attempts to assert themselves as adults.

These attempts usually create quite a bit of tension in the home, largely because teenagers aren't yet capable of living as adults. They still expect to be fed breakfast, lunch, and dinner. They expect to have their clothes washed, dried, ironed, and folded. They expect to use the family car even when they don't have money to pay for gas.

In other words, in their efforts to establish themselves as individuals, teenagers often claim the benefits and privileges of their homes even as they attempt to isolate themselves from their families. They attempt to live as individuals in the midst of community.

How did you attempt to establish your individuality as a teenager?

There's a similar dynamic at play in the church today. Because we live in an individualistic society, it's easy for us as Christians to lose sight of the fact that we're supposed to be bonded together as a church. We're supposed to act as members of the same body who are spiritually linked together to achieve the same purpose—to function as living stones who are willingly joined to serve as the foundation of God's kingdom in this world.

Instead, we typically think of Christianity in terms of individual justification, sanctification, and glorification. We focus on what living as a Christian means for us personally rather than concentrating on our role as members of the church. In other words, we lean toward self-centeredness even as we attempt to follow Christ.

What's your reaction to the previous statements?

If you're a believer in Jesus Christ, He has a purpose for you here on earth that's much bigger than your individual salvation. You've been reborn into a community of believers, and God expects you to function as a vital member of that community. Therefore, you need to understand and practice the vital doctrine of unity in the church.

# THE NEED FOR UNITY

During Jesus' last supper with His disciples in the upper room, He prayed what we refer to today as the High Priestly Prayer, a lovely, poignant interaction between Jesus and His Father. In the middle of that prayer, Jesus interceded for His followers in the room:

> *I am no longer in the world; and yet they themselves are in the world,*
> *and I come to You. Holy Father, keep them in Your name, the name*
> *which You have given Me, that they may be one even as We are.*
> JOHN 17:11

In the same way, Jesus prayed for all of His followers who would come later in history, including you and me:

> *I do not ask on behalf of these [the apostles] alone, but for those also who believe in*
> *Me through their word; that they may all be one; even as You, Father, are in Me and*
> *I in You, that they also may be in Us, so that the world may believe that You sent Me.*
> *The glory which You have given Me I have given to them, that they may be one, just*
> *as We are one; I in them and You in Me, that they may be perfected in unity, so that*
> *the world may know that You sent Me, and loved them, even as You have loved Me.*
> JOHN 17:20-23

How would you summarize Jesus' intercession on behalf of His followers?

How does Jesus' prayer contribute to your understanding of unity in the church?

Do you see the emphasis Jesus placed on unity in the church? "The glory which You have given Me I have given to them, *that they may be one*" (v. 22, emphasis added). Do you see how much is at stake when it comes to unity in the church? "I in them and You in Me, that they may be perfected in unity, *so that the world may know that You sent Me*" (v. 23, emphasis added).

Our bond as believers in Christ is much more than something designed to keep us from fussing and fighting among ourselves. It goes beyond avoiding conflict in the church. Instead, our unity as a collection of Christians serves as a testimony to the world that the God and the faith we preach are real.

Why does unity between Christians have such an impact in the world?

Where have you seen Christians unified in an effort to carry out God's kingdom agenda?

## THE SOURCE OF UNITY

You've probably heard that oil and water don't mix. That's true unless something else is brought into the mix. Take mayonnaise, for example. Water and soybean oil are two of the primary ingredients in mayonnaise, so how do the manufacturers get them to mix?

The answer is an emulsifier. To make mayonnaise, you must use an emulsifying ingredient—in this case, eggs—that can reach out to the water and oil and bind them together. In other words, the emulsifier prevents all of the different ingredients from going their own ways.

Similarly, the Holy Spirit is the divine emulsifier in the church. His role is to bind people together in the family of God—people of different races, ages, social classes, financial situations, and so on. Here's how Paul explained the Spirit's role in building church unity:

> *Even as the body is one and yet has many members, and all the members*
> *of the body, though they are many, are one body, so also is Christ. For by*
> *one Spirit we were all baptized into one body, whether Jews or Greeks,*
> *whether slaves or free, and we were all made to drink of one Spirit.*
> 1 CORINTHIANS 12:12-13

What do these verses teach about the church?

There's a flipside to this equation—one that doesn't paint a pleasant picture of the modern church. Because if the Holy Spirit's role is to promote unity in the church, what do we say about a church that's currently experiencing disunity? What do we say when individual congregations experience division and segregation?

We know the Holy Spirit isn't letting us down or failing to do His job. Therefore, the only answer is that we aren't relying on the Spirit in our efforts to live together as the church. In fact, we work against the Spirit (and against God's kingdom agenda) when we refuse to work together as individuals and congregations in the body of Christ.

What's your response to the previous statements?

What barriers are currently preventing you from experiencing a greater level of unity with other members of the church?

While disunity causes damage in the church, unity brings both power and productivity. The early church understood the power of a unified body of believers. That's why when local authorities threatened the apostles, the people of the church came together and "lifted their voices to God with one accord" (Acts 4:24). What happened next was astonishing.

Read Acts 4:24-31. What were the results when the entire congregation joined together in prayer?

As members of the church, we have an opportunity to boldly proclaim the gospel of Jesus Christ in such a way that the very foundations of our culture are shaken and transformed—but only if we're in it together. Only through unity in the church can we as individuals and congregations truly advance God's kingdom agenda in this world.

# CHURCH MEMBERSHIP

"I don't have to go to church to be saved." "I don't have to belong to a church to be a Christian." "I can worship God in my home." Have you heard any of these statements given as an excuse by people who don't want to go to church? I certainly have.

> In what situations have you heard similar statements?

> When have you experienced seasons of life when you weren't enthusiastic about being part of a church?

It can be difficult to refute statements like these because they happen to be true—up to a point. The Bible makes it abundantly clear that Jesus Christ is the only way to salvation (see John 14:6). No organization can make you a Christian.

So what, then, is the value of church membership? Are Christians required to be members of a local body of believers? Is being part of a local church even helpful?

> How would you answer the previous questions?

We're going to explore these themes today, beginning with an important passage of Scripture from the Book of Hebrews.

## THE IMPORTANCE OF CHURCH MEMBERSHIP

The Book of Hebrews was originally a letter written to a group of Jewish believers facing severe persecution from local authorities, both political and religious. Because of that persecution these believers were on the verge of defecting from the Christian faith.

In his letter the author of Hebrews wrote three admonitions to aid the believers in their struggle. Here are the first two:

*Let us draw near with a sincere heart in full assurance of faith, having our hearts*
*sprinkled clean from an evil conscience and our bodies washed with pure water. Let us*
*hold fast the confession of our hope without wavering, for He who promised is faithful.*
HEBREWS 10:22-23

The first admonition was "Let us draw near" (v. 22). And from the context of verses 19-21, we know the author was encouraging his readers to draw near to "the holy place" (v. 19) and "the house of God" (v. 21). Through Christ each of us has direct access to the throne room of God. Therefore, it's tragic to have such a privilege in our grasp and fail to approach God with the confidence described in verse 22.

To be a Christian is to maintain a vertical, personal relationship with God.

How do you typically draw near to God?

The second admonition was "Let us hold fast the confession of our hope without wavering" (v. 23). In other words, "Don't back down and don't be ashamed of your faith." The author of Hebrews was exhorting his readers to be public about their faith in Christ and to stand firm even in the face of persecution.

Even today too many Christians are excited about Jesus on Sunday morning because it involves no risk, while Monday morning is a different story. How disappointing. We're children of the King; we should never look down on our royal heritage.

When have you recently had an opportunity to publicly declare your faith in Jesus? What happened?

The third admonition highlights the importance of membership in a local church:

*Let us consider how to stimulate one another to love and good deeds, not*
*forsaking our own assembling together, as is the habit of some, but encouraging*
*one another; and all the more as you see the day drawing near.*
HEBREWS 10:24-25

This is the meat of the message. If we want to survive spiritually in the midst of a culture that's hostile to God's kingdom agenda, we must approach His throne with confidence, we must live the Christian life with boldness, and we must "stimulate one another to love and good deeds, not forsaking our own assembling together."

Why do you need your local church? Because your relationship to the corporate body of Christians is crucial to your personal relationship with God. Indeed, your connection with your local church is a key element that can prevent you from regressing spiritually or abandoning your faith altogether. That's because the relationships in your local church provide encouragement and support as you approach God's throne and attempt to live boldly as a follower of Christ.

How has your church helped you draw near to God?

How has your church helped you to "hold fast the confession of [your] hope without wavering" (v. 23)?

You don't need the local church to be saved. You don't need the local church to worship God. But you do need the local church to live according to God's kingdom agenda. I say that not only because God has commanded all Christians to gather in local assemblies (see v. 25) but also because all of us need encouragement, support, and even correction as we seek to follow Jesus in a world that's hostile to Him and His agenda.

## WHAT IT MEANS TO BE A CHURCH MEMBER

Different churches have different standards and processes for becoming an official member, but the core idea is the same. Church membership can be defined this way:

**CHURCH MEMBERSHIP:** THE COMMITMENT TO BE IDENTIFIED AND DYNAMICALLY INVOLVED WITH A LOCAL BODY OF BELIEVERS WHO ARE GROWING TOGETHER AS DISCIPLES OF JESUS CHRIST

What's your response to that definition?

What's your current membership status in your church?

Being a member of a local church has many benefits, both practical and spiritual. Participation in the life of a church offers regular opportunities for worship, fellowship, education, and outreach—all necessary activities for genuinely following God's kingdom agenda. Church membership offers the opportunity to experience God's glory (see Eph. 3:21) and to receive personal support and care from God's people (see 1 Cor. 12:25).

What other benefits have you received from participation and membership in a local church?

Unfortunately, one problem threatening the productivity of churches today is Christians who live by what I refer to as cruise-ship membership. The main reason I enjoy cruises is that somebody else does everything for you. You don't even have to handle your luggage. The ship's crew cleans your quarters, arranges your recreation, and provides you with great food for about eight meals a day. Every detail on a cruise ship is designed to pamper the participants on board.

That's great for a vacation, but it's bad for a church. Too many Christians say, "I'll cruise on over to church this morning and see what it has for me. I'll check out the music menu and take a few samples from the sermon buffet."

How have you seen a cruise-ship mentality present in the church today?

The truth is that a local church is supposed to operate like a battleship instead of a cruise ship. You know what the captain says on a battleship when the enemy is about to be engaged: "All hands to battle stations." Every person on a battleship is expected to earn his keep by doing a job that's vital to the ship's operation and to ultimate victory in battle.

That's our call as members of a church: "All hands to battle stations."

What are some tasks and responsibilities necessary for operating a victorious church?

How do you participate in the life and ultimate victory of your church?

One way we're called to serve as church members is by using our God-given gifts to build up the body of Christ and serve the kingdom of God. Let me be clear: there's no such thing as a Christian who doesn't serve the kingdom by ministering to the church. Just as your physical body can't live without all of your members doing their individual jobs, the body of Christ can't live without all of us doing our part.

What gifts have you been given that can be used in the church?

Read the following passages of Scripture and record what they teach about using our gifts as members of the church.

1 Corinthians 12:1-12

1 Peter 4:9-11

We as church members also have a privilege and responsibility to contribute financially to the work of God's kingdom through our local churches. I know that's not always a popular topic, but it's biblical:

> *Concerning the collection for the saints, as I directed the churches of Galatia,*
> *so do you also. On the first day of every week each one of you is to put aside*
> *and save, as he may prosper, so that no collections be made when I come.*
> 1 CORINTHIANS 16:1-2

How satisfied are you with your current level of financial giving to God through your church? Explain.

When you know you're on the winning team, you can afford to give it everything you've got. As a follower of Christ, you're privileged to enjoy the benefits of your local church, and you're called to advance the kingdom of God through its ministry.

So jump in! Serve, give, and work through the church even as you enjoy the fellowship, support, and teaching of the church. Anything less is unworthy of God's kingdom agenda.

# THE CHURCH'S CALL TO OUTREACH

This week we've looked at both the nature and the purpose of the church. We've also explored what it means to live and minister as members of the church, both locally and universally. I hope you've developed an appreciation for the way the church allows us as Christians to operate in two worlds at the same time.

After all, the church is made up of people called to live out heaven's values in the midst of an unheavenly culture. We receive instructions from above, yet our feet are firmly planted below. We're called to think heavenly thoughts even as we allow those thoughts to work themselves out in our earthly walk.

In short, we as members of the church are longing for the return of Jesus, our King, but we have a lot of work to do while we wait for His arrival.

> In what situations are you most aware of the tension between your earthly life and your heavenly calling?

> How does the church help you manage that tension?

As we await the return of Christ, part of our work involves the growth of men, women, and children who are already members of the church. This task includes discipleship, spiritual growth, unity, membership, and other themes we've already touched on this week.

But another part of our work involves the impact we make externally in the lives of those currently outside the church. That's why I'd like to conclude this week by focusing on the importance of outreach in today's society.

## SALT AND LIGHT

During the Sermon on the Mount, Jesus made a concise yet comprehensive statement on how the church is supposed to influence society. He used two metaphors to communicate the impact He wants us as the church to make on His behalf. Here's the first:

*You are the salt of the earth; but if the salt has become tasteless,*
*how can it be made salty again? It is no longer good for anything,*
*except to be thrown out and trampled under foot by men.*
MATTHEW 5:13

To understand Jesus' words, we need to recognize the importance of salt as the primary preservative in the ancient world. Because salt is antibacterial, rubbing it into a piece of meat helped to preserve that meat from decay, thus extending its usefulness as a source of sustenance for a family. In a world without refrigeration, salt was essential.

When Jesus referred to His followers as "the salt of the earth," He expressed two important implications.

## 1. JESUS IMPLIED THAT THE WORLD OF HIS DAY WAS IN A SERIOUS STATE OF DETERIORATION. After all, why would the

world need salt unless it required preserving? Why send out antibacterial agents unless there's the potential for decay? The world was rotting under the influence of sin during Jesus' day, and things have only gotten worse as the centuries have passed.

Where do you see evidence of deterioration and decay in today's society?

## 2. JESUS IMPLIED THAT HIS FOLLOWERS CAN PLAY AN IMPORTANT ROLE AS AGENTS OF PRESERVATION. If Jesus

didn't have any work for us here on earth, He would have already brought us to Himself. Instead, our King has intentionally placed us in our world and in our individual spheres of life to function as salt—to be preserving influences in a rotting world. We as the church have the task of slowing down the decay of sin.

However, salt can't do its job when it stays in the saltshaker. In order to fulfill our role as agents of preservation, we must open the doors of the church and go out into the world to spread the salt of God's kingdom wherever it's needed. If we want to preserve our families, communities, and nation against the corruption of sin, the salt must be at work.

In what ways does your church intentionally engage and influence your broader community?

Another key feature of salt is that it produces thirst when consumed. That's why peanuts, pretzels, and other salty snacks are often free at restaurants. You're supposed to eat a bunch of free snacks so that you'll eventually say, "I need to buy a drink."

In the same way, the job of the church is to create the kind of thirst in the culture that can be satisfied only by the living water of Jesus Christ. We don't have to worry about making Christianity attractive or palatable in the world. We just need to worry about living under God's kingdom agenda and reflecting the values of His kingdom to such a degree that people become thirsty for Jesus.

Can you think of anyone at work, at school, or in your neighborhood who's become thirsty for the living water simply because your life and your church are so salty for Christ?

What's your answer to the previous question?

If you're living as the salt of the earth, but you're not producing thirst in the lives of those who come in contact with you, then something's wrong. You're in danger of becoming tasteless, and tasteless salt is good for nothing "except to be thrown out and trampled under foot by men."

What steps can you take to become more salty in your everyday life?

Let's look at Jesus' second metaphor, which we briefly explored earlier in this study:

> *You are the light of the world. A city set on a hill cannot be hidden; nor does anyone light a lamp and put it under a basket, but on the lampstand, and it gives light to all who are in the house. Let your light shine before men in such a way that they may see your good works, and glorify your Father who is in heaven.*
> MATTHEW 5:14-16

In the same way that salt preserves against corruption, the nature of light is to drive away darkness—but only when used properly. Light is useless when it's kept hidden, just as we in the church are useless unless we make our way out into the darkness of the world to reflect the glory of Christ.

What tensions or obstacles cause you to hide your light as a Christian?

How can you move past those barriers to properly reflect the light and glory of Christ?

## MOVING OUT

Will you fulfill your role as salt and light in your family? In your community? In your country and the world at large? If so, you'll need to start by moving out of your comfort zone and by identifying areas in which you can have an impact.

There are people in your community right now who are dying from the corruption and decay caused by sin—maybe people in your own family. Will you go out and be salt for those people, or will you be tasteless? In the same way, there are places in your community where hunger, sickness, and despair run rampant under the cover of darkness. Will you be a light in those places, or will you remain hidden?

What specific need or difficult situation came to mind when you read the previous paragraph?

How will you intentionally address that need or situation this week as salt and light?

As a follower of Jesus, you're a vital member of the body of Christ. You're part of the church, so you've been called to reflect the values of God's kingdom and actively work to advance His agenda throughout the different spheres of your life.

Will you answer that call?

Week 5

# ONE NATION UNDER GOD

# START

**Welcome back to this small-group discussion of Kingdom Agenda.**

Last week's application challenge asked you to pray daily for your church, as well as for the other churches in your community. If you're comfortable, talk about your experiences and any insights you gained through prayer.

Describe what you liked best in the material from week 4. What questions do you have?

How have the members of your church effectively served as salt and light to make a difference in your community?

How do you react or respond when you hear the phrase "One nation under God"?

To prepare for the DVD segment, read aloud the following verses.

> *For many days Israel was without the true God and without a teaching priest and without law. But in their distress they turned to the LORD God of Israel, and they sought Him, and He let them find Him. In those times there was no peace to him who went out or to him who came in, for many disturbances afflicted all the inhabitants of the lands. Nation was crushed by nation, and city by city, for God troubled them with every kind of distress.*
> 2 CHRONICLES 15:3-6

# WATCH

**Complete the viewer guide below as you watch DVD session 5.**

Government was created by _____.

If God is your problem, only God is your _____.

The closer God is to a society, the more _____ the society will be. The further God is, the more _____ society will be.

God intended men under His government to live in _____.

When you do not allow God to be God, men will seek their authority from another source and put men in _____.

God says to government, "If you operate under My covenant, you get the benefits of My _____."

The goal of civil government is to maintain a safe, just, and righteous environment for _____ to flourish.

God will allow a culture to _____ Him until it learns its lesson that it can't live without Him.

Government was never supposed to operate independently of _____.

When you have the right _____ and when you apply those principles, government is reflecting or mirroring God.

Servants of the people are supposed to be _____ of God.

High taxation means big government. Freedom allows for _____ taxation.

# RESPOND

*Use the following questions to discuss the DVD segment with your group.*

What did you appreciate most in Dr. Evans's teaching? Why?

What are some specific descriptive words you would use to describe our country?

Respond to Dr. Evans's statement: "The closer God is to a society, the more ordered the society will be. The further God is from society, the more chaotic society will be. So if you want an ordered society, keep God close."

How do we keep God close in today's society?

What entities, ideas, or values in our society are actively working to push God away?

How would you summarize the role of government in relation to God's kingdom agenda?

What steps can we take as Christians to advance God's kingdom through our culture and our country's political processes?

**Application.** Continue last week's commitment to intercessory prayer, but this week focus on your country. Whenever you see a news report or a headline with national implications, pray that God will use His people and His church to advance His kingdom agenda throughout modern society.

**This week's Scripture memory.**

*He has told you, O man, what is good;*
*And what does the LORD require of you*
*But to do justice, to love kindness,*
*And to walk humbly with your God?*
MICAH 6:8

**Assignment.** Read week 5 and complete the activities before the next group experience.

## CITIZENS OF TWO KINGDOMS

It's possible in the world today to achieve a status known as dual citizenship. This occurs when a person is legally and officially recognized as a citizen of two separate nations, and it's allowed to happen because different nations have different ways of determining citizenship within their borders.

Many nations confer citizenship based on a principle known as *jus soli*—the right of the soil. If a child is born within the boundaries of these nations, he or she is automatically considered a citizen. In other words, citizenship comes through birth.

Other nations are willing to confer citizenship based on *jus sanguinis*—the right of the blood. In these nations people can be recognized as citizens simply because their parents were citizens. This is true even if the prospective citizens weren't born in that country, and it can occur even when the prospective citizens don't live in that country.

People can also achieve dual citizenship through legal channels. If you marry a citizen of a particular country, for example, you're often granted citizenship in that country because of your spouse. Or you can go through the process of naturalization by living and working in a country while you apply for citizenship.

As followers of Jesus Christ, we've been granted dual citizenship in a spiritual sense. We live here on earth and are citizens of an earthly nation, yet we're also citizens of God's kingdom according to both *jus soli* and *jus sanguinis;* we're born again into the kingdom of God through the blood of Jesus Christ.

Being a citizen of two kingdoms can create tension. What do we do when the precepts and values of our earthly home conflict with the values and precepts of God's reign? How do we operate as citizens of two kingdoms when the very foundations of those kingdoms clash over important issues, ideas, and priorities?

These are the themes we'll explore this week as we focus on the way God's kingdom agenda influences our participation in our community and our nation.

## *Day 1*
# FREEDOM IN THE KINGDOM

I love New York City. If I could choose anywhere in America to visit for a week, I'd choose New York. One thing I've always appreciated most about New York City is its diversity. Walking down the crowded streets, riding in a cab, or stopping in a store or restaurant takes you across the path of people from a wide variety of cultural backgrounds.

It's no surprise that the Big Apple is filled with so many different groups of people. After all, there's a lady standing in the main harbor whose crown has seven spikes representing the seven seas and the seven continents of the world. For more than a century she's been inviting the inhabitants of the world to come to America, and a plaque mounted inside the lower portion of her pedestal includes these words:

> *Give me your tired, your poor,*
> *Your huddled masses yearning to breathe free,*
> *The wretched refuse of your teeming shore,*
> *Send these, the homeless, tempest-tossed to me,*
> *I lift my lamp beside the golden door.*

I love that phrase "yearning to breathe free." Lady Liberty proclaims freedom every day to anyone with a heart to hear. She represents the foundation of freedom, justice, and equality on which America was built and has been maintained—although sometimes imperfectly—for centuries.

Sadly, although the opportunity to experience legal and religious freedom still exists in America today, many people choose to live in bondage. They willingly allow themselves to be shackled by chains of injustice in many forms—economic injustice, racial injustice, educational injustice, vocational injustice, and more.

In what ways do you see people choosing bondage instead of freedom?

How have you been able to break away from bondage in the past?

This week we're going to look at these and other forms of injustice as we explore the implications of God's kingdom agenda for our nation. Today, however, I'd like to highlight some of the nuances and possibilities implied by the word *freedom.* I want to focus not only on how freedom pertains to us as a nation but also on how it affects us as individuals who form the bedrock of our society.

What ideas or images come to mind when you hear the word *freedom?*

## WHAT IS FREEDOM?

For an ideal that's referenced and revered so often in our society, freedom can be difficult to define. When I look up the word *freedom* in dictionaries and encyclopedias, much of what I read sounds incomplete and ambiguous. The true depth and meaning of this word—for which many people have died and many more have hoped—are difficult to express.

When we approach freedom from a biblical perspective, however, it's a little easier to pin down. So here's my definition of *freedom* from the Tony Evans Dictionary:

**FREEDOM:** A RELEASE FROM ILLEGITIMATE
BONDAGE THAT ALLOWS PEOPLE TO CHOOSE
TO EXERCISE RESPONSIBILITY IN MAXIMIZING
ALL THEY WERE CREATED TO BE

How would you rewrite the previous definition in your own words?

The most important thing we need to understand about freedom is that it originated with God. Freedom is and has always been God's idea, and He's offered it as a priceless gift to human beings. In fact, freedom was one of the themes God spoke about with Adam before sin entered the world:

> The LORD God took the man and put him into the garden of Eden to cultivate it and keep it. The LORD God commanded the man, saying, **"From any tree of the garden you may eat freely;** but from the tree of the knowledge of good and evil you shall not eat, for in the day that you eat from it you will surely die."*
> GENESIS 2:15-17, emphasis added

People often interpret God's command to Adam as being restrictive. They read it as God's restricting Adam's right to eat whatever he wanted, thus limiting his freedom. In reality, nothing could be further from the truth. God said, "From any tree of the garden you may eat freely" (v. 16)—except one. God granted Adam a great deal of freedom.

This leads to a principle to keep in mind as we seek to understand the concept of freedom:

## TRUE FREEDOM INVOLVES THE MAXIMUM OPPORTUNITY TO ENJOY AND PARTAKE OF WHATEVER GOD LEGITIMATELY PROVIDES.

If God has blessed you with an abundance, you're free to partake of that abundance in accordance with His kingdom agenda.

In what areas of life has God granted you an abundance of blessings?

What emotions do you experience when you partake of those blessings?

Here's another principle to remember:

## FREEDOM DOESN'T IMPLY A LACK OF RESTRICTIONS.

As we've seen, God restricted Adam from eating the fruit of one tree even as He blessed Adam with an abundance of food from other sources. God was the source of both the freedom and the restriction, and both were good. In other words, freedom always comes with boundaries, because boundaries are an essential element of actually realizing and enjoying freedom.

Think about this: a tennis player wouldn't be free to play tennis if there were no base line. Baseball players wouldn't be free to play baseball if there were no foul lines; the game couldn't exist without those boundaries. A fish isn't free to roam in the jungle, nor is a lion free to live in the ocean.

The reason God has placed boundaries in our lives and our world is to create opportunities for us to take full advantage of our freedom. Without those boundaries we'd have chaos.

What are some boundaries in our society that actually promote freedom?

Here's the final principle we need to consider in order to fully understand the concept of freedom as God designed it:

## FREEDOM IS ALWAYS CONNECTED WITH CONSEQUENCES.

Adam wasn't created as a mindless robot; he had the freedom to disobey God's command. But notice the consequence of that disobedience: "In the day that you eat from it you will surely die" (Gen. 2:17).

God's kingdom operates by God's rules, and when those rules are broken—whether by individuals, families, churches, or nations—He enacts the appropriate consequences.

Where do you see the consequences of rebellion against God displayed in today's culture?

We live in a nation founded on the concept of freedom, yet so many people in our culture disregard God's boundaries, insist on unrestricted freedom, and then complain when consequences arise because they've exercised their freedom. Indeed, the cultural chaos we're experiencing today is directly connected to the failure of our society to abide by God's prescribed boundaries even as we enjoy the freedom He's given us.

In order to combat that chaos, we must return to the truth.

## FREEDOM AND TRUTH

During Jesus' time on earth, He delivered a singularly profound statement on the nature of freedom—a statement that not only applies to personal freedom but also establishes a framework for how a society can both experience and offer freedom at large. Here it is:

> *Jesus was saying to those Jews who had believed Him, "If you*
> *continue in My word, then you are truly disciples of Mine; and you*
> *will know the truth, and the truth will make you free."*
> JOHN 8:31-32

In verse 33 the people argued with Jesus, claiming they were already free. This was a ridiculous statement, since the entire population of Israel had been under Roman rule for centuries. Nevertheless, Jesus chose not to engage their arguments. Instead, He outlined the way for them to experience true freedom:

> *Jesus answered them, "Truly, truly, I say to you, everyone who commits sin is the slave of sin. The slave does not remain in the house forever; the son does remain forever. So if the Son makes you free, you will be free indeed."*
> JOHN 8:34-36

First Jesus said, "If you continue in My word, ... the truth will make you free" (vv. 31-32). Then He said, "If the Son makes you free, you will be free indeed" (v. 36). The path is clear. If we want to experience the benefits of freedom—as individuals or as a nation—we must look to the truth of God's Word, and we must return to the source of truth, Jesus Christ.

How have you experienced freedom through your study of God's Word?

How have you experienced freedom through your relationship with Jesus?

Sadly, one of the leading causes of spiritual defeat and bondage in our nation (and in the world at large) is that people have decided to trust what they feel over what God says. Too many people use their personal feelings to define their reality; they seek freedom in their own emotions, experiences, and desires instead of in God's truth.

In what areas of life are you trusting your feelings and experiences more than the truth of God's Word?

We must turn away from our current trajectory. There is a direct correlation between the preeminence given to Christ as King in a person's life and the freedom that person experiences. In the same way, the degree to which Jesus is exalted in families, churches, and communities is the same degree to which the rivers of genuine, biblical freedom will flow through our land.

# JUSTICE IN THE KINGDOM

As we saw yesterday, freedom is a critical building block in God's kingdom. For that reason a major component of God's kingdom agenda includes promoting and advancing throughout the world the true freedom that can be found only in Christ.

People inside and outside the church often use the term *social justice* to describe attempts to spread freedom by eliminating injustice and by promoting positive lifestyles. However, in recent years that term has become convoluted, so it can mean different things to different people. For example, it's often used as a catchphrase for illegitimate forms of government that promote the redistribution of wealth and the continued expansion of civil authority—systems that wrongly infringe on the jurisdiction of the family and the church.

What ideas or images come to mind when you hear the term *justice?*

What ideas or images come to mind when you hear the term *social justice?*

To avoid confusion, we'll use the term *biblical justice* in this study as we explore our responsibility as Christians to promote and advance freedom in our society. This will allow us to focus on God's Word as we seek to understand the meaning and importance of justice in connection with God's kingdom agenda.

## UNDERSTANDING JUSTICE

The various terms translated *justice* in the Bible generally carry the meaning of prescribing something in the right way. They refer to ruling or exercising authority in a way that's both appropriate and effective. Therefore, the concept of justice is intimately tied to God, who is the ultimate Ruler of all things.

In fact, the only way we can understand whether something is just or unjust is by comparing it to God, who's perfectly just:

*The Rock! His work is perfect,*
*For all His ways are just;*
*A God of faithfulness and without injustice,*
*Righteous and upright is He.*
DEUTERONOMY 32:4

God is "without injustice." Therefore, He's the only Being qualified to make the laws and boundaries that apply universally throughout creation:

*There is only one Lawgiver and Judge, the One who is able to save*
*and to destroy; but who are you who judge your neighbor?*
JAMES 4:12

How would you summarize the connection between God and justice?

Read the following passages of Scripture and record what they teach about the concept of justice.

Leviticus 19:15-16

Deuteronomy 16:18-20

Psalm 111:7-8

Based on these biblical teachings, here's my definition of *biblical justice* from the Tony Evans Dictionary:

## BIBLICAL JUSTICE: THE EQUITABLE AND IMPARTIAL APPLICATION OF THE RULE OF GOD'S MORAL LAW IN SOCIETY

As individuals, families, and churches, we operate justly when we seek to apply God's moral law across all areas of life. We operate unjustly and promote injustice when we deviate from God's law and rely on our own desires or on the ever-changing waters of cultural opinion.

On a national level, governments around the world are supposed to serve as instruments of divine justice by impartially establishing, reflecting, and applying God's divine standards of justice in society. When that fails to happen, we experience the kind of moral chaos currently on display in modern culture.

How do you evaluate our government according to the previous standards?

Let me emphasize this point before we move on: it's *not* God's desire to see a separation between the spiritual and social aspects of our society—between the sacred and the secular. In fact, the Bible expressly states that the reason for social disintegration and all kinds of immorality in a culture can be traced back to people who wrongfully remove spirituality from their everyday lives (see 2 Chron. 15:3-6).

What's your reaction to the previous statements? Why?

When God created human beings, He gave us the responsibility to rule the earth under His divine authority while simultaneously spreading His image throughout the world (see Gen. 1:26-28). Our subsequent refusal to submit to divine authority first led to social disintegration. When Adam and Eve disobeyed God, the results were family breakdown, economic struggle, emotional instability, and physical death (see Gen. 3:1-19).

In other words, the closer God's rule is reflected in a society—even in the elements of society that are traditionally considered secular—the more ordered and productive that society will be. If God's rule and spiritual values are removed from society, however, the result will be chaos.

Where do you see divisions between the spiritual and social aspects of modern society?

How have you contributed to or participated in those divisions?

Biblical justice isn't a man-made, socially imposed, top-down system of government that ultimately leads to the restriction of freedom. Rather, to strive for biblical justice in our nation is to promote freedom by emphasizing accountability, equality, and responsibility *because* of the nature of God and His kingdom.

## OUR GOD OF JUSTICE

Not only is God the standard by which we understand justice, but He's also repeatedly described throughout Scripture as One who delivers justice and defends the cause of those throughout the world who need justice.

For example, the exodus from Egypt dramatically portrays God's execution of biblical justice on behalf of the Israelites, a people group that experienced extreme levels of injustice and oppression. In a similar way, God later charged the Israelites with maintaining justice in society because of the deliverance they'd received:

> *You shall not wrong a stranger or oppress him, for you were strangers in the land of Egypt. You shall not afflict any widow or orphan. If you afflict him at all, and if he does cry out to Me, I will surely hear his cry.*
> EXODUS 22:21-23

Read the following passages of Scripture and record what they teach about God as an active advocate for justice.

1 Kings 3:16-28

Amos 5:21-24

Zechariah 7:8-14

What common themes characterize the previous passages?

God is an active deliverer and defender of justice. Therefore, the role of the church and of individual Christians is to execute divine justice in the world as part of God's kingdom agenda. It should also be noted that Scripture continually calls us to seek justice on behalf of the poor, defenseless, and oppressed. These groups are a primary concern because they represent segments of society that typically bear the brunt of injustices.

For example, God's Word forbids mistreating the poor (see Jas. 2:15-16) and demonstrating prejudice based on race or class (see Gal. 2:11-14). Rather, we as Christians are called to meet the physical, emotional, and spiritual needs of the have-nots in our culture.

How does your church promote justice for the have-nots in society?

On a scale of 1 to 10, how satisfied are you with your own participation in these efforts?

| 1 | 2 | 3 | 4 | 5 | 6 | 7 | 8 | 9 | 10 |
|---|---|---|---|---|---|---|---|---|----|
| Not satisfied | | | | | | | | | Very satisfied |

I want to emphasize again that biblical justice isn't simply a good idea or a nice program in the church. It's a command of our King. In fact, it's a primary component of one of the most powerful summaries of the Christian life contained in God's Word:

> *He has told you, O man, what is good;*
> *And what does the LORD require of you*
> *But to do justice, to love kindness,*
> *And to walk humbly with your God?*
> MICAH 6:8

Christians "do justice" in a humble relationship with a just God as a natural reflection of His presence in our lives. In other words, religion becomes authentic when it manifests itself in ministry to others in need.

What will you do this week to intentionally seek justice for the helpless as an expression of your relationship with God?

In the same way, "to do justice" is to fulfill Jesus' Great Commandment that we love God and love others as we seek to follow Him (see Matt. 22:37-40). Jesus connected our attitude toward God (spiritual) with our attitude and actions toward others (social). Both are essential in living out God's kingdom agenda.

Tomorrow we'll focus on what it actually looks like to implement biblical justice in the church and in our nation as a whole.

# IMPLEMENTING BIBLICAL JUSTICE

We have a ministry of justice in the church I pastor in Dallas. Run by fully qualified legal representatives, this ministry uses a process to render decisions in our congregation on issues like marital disputes, business lawsuits, juvenile delinquency, restitution, divorce, and so on.

Does that sound strange to you? Does that sound like a poor use of the church's resources? Does that sound as if our church is overreaching our authority in a state (and nation) with a fully equipped police force and legal system?

What's your response to the previous questions?

If you answered yes to any of the previous questions, you still have a few things to learn about implementing biblical justice in your life as an individual, in your city or community, and in your church.

Let me give you an example of the way our justice ministry works on a practical level. A young man in our church—I'll call him Chris—stole $1,500 from his employer a few years ago. He was eventually caught, arrested, and on the verge of being locked up in jail for three years—at a cost of about $18,000 a year to the taxpayers of our community. In addition to that cost, Chris would have come out of prison in three years as a more highly trained criminal, and his employer would never have seen a dime of the stolen money.

I sent a group of men from our church to the judge over Chris's case. We said, "Your Honor, if you'll release Chris into our care, we'll assign upstanding men to be responsible for him, find him a job, garnish his wages, and pay back his former employer." The judge agreed to our terms, and we carried them out.

Six months later we took Chris back to the judge and showed him what had happened. Chris was under the influence of godly men, had found a reliable job, had repaid the stolen money to his previous employer, and was finally taking responsibility for his actions.

The judge was astonished. In fact, a little while later he called us and said, "Will you take 20 more like Chris and do the same thing?"

How does Chris's story serve as an example of biblical justice?

Do you think it's realistic for your church to actively pursue biblical justice in a similar way? Explain.

The church must be a place where biblical justice is not only proclaimed but also modeled and carried out for the benefit of society at large. With that in mind, today we'll focus on three key principles for implementing biblical justice in the world: restitution, reconciliation, and responsibility.

## BIBLICAL RESTITUTION

One concept that separates biblical justice from our modern legal system is that biblical justice emphasizes restitution for the victim in addition to punishment for the crime. When a wrong has been committed in society, biblical justice seeks to repair the damage that was caused and to prevent future damage, not just to punish the wrongdoer.

Here's an example of restitution from the Old Testament:

> *If a man lets a field or vineyard be grazed bare and lets his animal*
> *loose so that it grazes in another man's field, he shall make restitution*
> *from the best of his own field and the best of his own vineyard.*
> EXODUS 22:5

How would you summarize the principle of restitution?

Obviously, this isn't a scenario that many of us will encounter today, but let's focus on the underlying principle: when we do wrong or promote injustice, we have a responsibility to make things right. The church can help in this regard.

As an objective body of believers committed to biblical justice, the church is the perfect entity to review conflicts and even crimes in an effort to ensure that restitution takes place whenever possible and the victims are defended.

When have you been a victim of wrongdoing and in need of restitution? What happened?

What steps could your church take to pursue a ministry of restitution in your community?

## BIBLICAL RECONCILIATION

Churches are also ideally positioned to help people work toward reconciliation in their communities. When injustice occurs, the consequences go beyond financial loss and legal recriminations. The relational component also needs to be resolved.

To put it simply, when people in a community commit wrongs against each other, they place severe strain on the relationships in that community. Over time this strain causes deep-seated bitterness, mistrust, and even prejudice. And when these relational divides are multiplied throughout a nation, people can no longer function together for the common good.

Where do you see examples of relational damage and mistrust in your community? In our society as a whole?

That's why Jesus said the following:

> *If you are presenting your offering at the altar, and there remember that your brother has something against you, leave your offering there before the altar and go; first be reconciled to your brother, and then come and present your offering.*
> MATTHEW 5:23-24

How do these verses contribute to your understanding of reconciliation?

Biblical justice goes beyond a legal resolution to conflict and injustice. It's a call to restore relationships both inside and outside the body of Christ.

# BIBLICAL RESPONSIBILITY

Finally, the church can help implement biblical justice in our communities and in our nation by helping people take responsibility for their actions and lifestyles. When you think of the terms commonly associated with social action, it's clear that our approach to dealing with injustice is temporary. We offer relief, charity, and aid.

Instead, we need to offer empowerment. Injustice is more than simply mistreating the poor or oppressing the helpless. Injustice also involves a refusal to appropriately equip and empower those who'd like to take control of their situation but can't. As the church, we must help victims of injustice find the power they need to ultimately and permanently take responsibility for their well-being and the health of their communities. We see these principles at work in the biblical concept of gleaning:

> *When you reap the harvest of your land, you shall not reap to the very corners of your field, nor shall you gather the gleanings of your harvest. Nor shall you glean your vineyard, nor shall you gather the fallen fruit of your vineyard; you shall leave them for the needy and for the stranger. I am the LORD your God.*
> LEVITICUS 19:9-10

Gleaning provided an opportunity for the poor and defenseless to help themselves through their own labor, thus preserving their dignity. It allowed people to turn poverty into productivity and ultimately transform their lives.

So how can the church do the same in our nation today? One option is to fight for and support economic systems that encourage productivity through responsibility, not maintain government-run welfare states that ultimately force people to endure injustice in order to receive charity. Another option is to come alongside the educational system and ensure that the children of injustice have access to knowledge that will allow them to fight for their own responsibility and well-being in the world.

You can explore my book *The Kingdom Agenda* and my website, *www.tonyevans.org,* to find concrete examples of how individuals, families, and churches are working to fight injustice through empowerment and responsibility.

What specific steps can you take to help people in your community achieve responsibility rather than settle for charity?

# RACISM AND THE KINGDOM

As is the case with most African-Americans, racism has certainly been apparent to me during my lifetime. I can remember riding in the car with my father when I was a boy and passing a White Tower restaurant in Baltimore, where I grew up. The White Tower was famous for its hamburgers, so I said, "Why don't we stop in there and get a burger?"

My father answered, "Because we can't go there. They don't allow Negroes there." That incident sparked a whole series of questions to my father because it was the first time I'd dealt with the new reality of racism. It wasn't the last time.

I remember the week of April 4, 1968, when Dr. Martin Luther King Jr. was assassinated. I was 17 years old. The event caused explosive race riots in our city, and I watched from our house window as row on row of national guardsmen lined up along our street. Later, when I was in college, my wife and I were turned away from a well-known church in Dallas while attempting to attend a worship service. We weren't welcome because of our race.

How have you been affected by racism?

Where do you see racism still prevalent in our culture today?

I've been affected by racism. And no matter the color of your skin, you've been affected by racism too, because racism isn't a personal issue; it's a national issue. The problem of racism pervades our society beyond black-and-white experiences. It's a stain on modern culture that refuses to be laundered out. Therefore, to understand and deal with the problem of racism, we need to get a kingdom perspective on the larger issue of race.

## THE ORIGIN OF THE RACES

We need to start with the origin of the races in our world because it's both the foundation of the problem and the source of the solution.

What have you been taught in school about the origin of the different races on our planet?

What have you been taught in church about the origin of the races?

A number of theories have been set forth through the years in regard to racial origins. I want to address two of the most popular—one secular and one religious—before I provide a biblical answer to the topic.

The Environmental Theory of racial origins states that racial differences can largely be explained by environment and geography. According to this view, Anglos have light skin because they settled in Europe, where they didn't experience extreme exposure to the sun. The people who settled in Africa, however, were closer to the equator and regularly exposed to intense sunlight, leading to darker skin.

What I refer to as the Curse of Ham Theory is another attempt to explain racial origins. This one is based on the account of Ham found in Genesis 9, following the flood of Noah.

Read Genesis 9:20-27. What are your initial reactions to this passage?

The thesis behind the Curse of Ham Theory is that Ham and his descendants were given the curse of living in perpetual slavery. And because Ham is the father of black people, black people have always been and are still under a divine curse of servitude.

This position has so many flaws that it's hard to know where to start. But the main thing to understand for the purposes of our current conversation is that Noah's curse wasn't directed at Ham, the father of African people groups. It was directed at Ham's youngest son, Canaan. So the claim that God somehow cursed all people of African descent is false.

Also remember that Canaan was the father of the Canaanites—the evil, pagan people living in the promised land when the Israelites arrived to take possession of what God had promised. God commanded the Israelites to eradicate the Canaanites as an expression of His judgment against their sin (see Josh. 9:23-25). The Israelites didn't do the job all at once, but eventually the Canaanites, as a nation, disappeared from the earth (see Zeph. 2:5). And the curse that Noah placed on them died with them.

In other words, any attempt to place the curse of Genesis 9 on every person of African descent is an inaccurate interpretation of God's Word.

How can we as Christians prevent inaccurate theories of racial origins
from causing further damage in the church and in society?

Here's a clearer and more accurate picture of racial origins in this world:

*He made from one man every nation of mankind to live on all the face of the earth,
having determined their appointed times and the boundaries of their habitation.*
ACTS 17:26

How does this verse contribute to your understanding of racial origins?

The question of racial origins has a one-word answer: God. We don't have different races
because of exposure to sunlight or because of a curse. Rather, God planned for and
designed the ethnic diversity of our world when He created Adam and Eve.

We can see the evidence of God's plan all the way back in Genesis 9. The sons of Noah
were named Ham, Shem, and Japheth. In the original language *Ham* means *hot, dark,
burnt,* which is why he's considered the father of black people. *Shem* means *brownish,
dusky,* and *Japheth* means, *fair, light.* So God's plan for ethnic diversity was already in
place when Noah's family began the work of repopulating the earth after the flood.

That means your color and mine aren't products of chance or nature. God created all
people from one. Therefore, there are no racial mistakes.

What emotions or reactions do you experience when you contemplate your
ethnicity? Why?

## MOVING TOWARD RECONCILIATION

*Racism* may be simply defined as *the discrimination of people based on skin color or
ethnic origin.* It involves the unrighteous use of power against people toward whom we
harbor prejudice, which is the emotional foundation for discrimination. Racism is equally
unrighteous when practiced by any people group against another. It's an affront to the
character of God, and the solution never involves practicing racism in reverse.

So how do we move forward? How do we solve the problem of racism both as a nation and as a body of believers?

One reason we've had so much trouble eliminating racism in our nation and in the church is that we continue to view it as a skin problem rather than a sin problem. When you believe racism is only a skin problem—that it's ultimately a misunderstanding based on external differences—you can spend three hundred years of slavery, court decisions, marches, and the federal government's involvement and still not fix it.

But when you see racism as a sin problem—when you understand that it's an affront to God and the values of His kingdom—then you're obligated as a believer to deal with it. At its core racism is a spiritual and theological issue, not merely a social or political problem.

What have Christians and churches done right in their attempts to solve the problem of racism?

The Bible offers a solution to the sin problem of racism, and we can see a picture of that solution in Galatians 2:11-13:

> When Cephas came to Antioch, I opposed him to his face, because he stood condemned. For prior to the coming of certain men from James, he used to eat with the Gentiles; but when they came, he began to withdraw and hold himself aloof, fearing the party of the circumcision. The rest of the Jews joined him in hypocrisy, with the result that even Barnabas was carried away by their hypocrisy.
> GALATIANS 2:11-13

How do these verses highlight the sinful nature of racism?

Prior to this incident Peter had been charged to spread the gospel to the Gentiles—people of a different ethnicity from his own—and even to eat the kinds of foods the Gentiles ate (see Acts 10:9-15). Peter obeyed and saw much spiritual fruit result.

But when Jewish believers from Jerusalem arrived, Peter made the mistake of engaging in racism by withdrawing from the Gentiles because he was afraid of the way the Jews would react. Worse, "the rest of the Jews joined him in hypocrisy" (v. 13). Peter, a leader in the church, led his people down the path of discrimination.

Fortunately, Paul chose not to be passive about racism. He confronted Peter, and in doing so, he put his finger on the solution for the racism we experience today:

> *When I saw that they were not straightforward about the truth of the gospel,*
> *I said to Cephas in the presence of all, "If you, being a Jew, live like the Gentiles*
> *and not like the Jews, how is it that you compel the Gentiles to live like Jews?"*
> GALATIANS 2:14

Today the kingdom solution to racism and the key to reconciliation are to be committed to the truth. Paul confronted Peter because he and the other Jews "were not straightforward about the truth of the gospel." And the truth of the gospel is that we're all one people in God's kingdom. In Christ "there is neither Jew nor Greek" (Gal. 3:28).

As Christians, we need to make two radical decisions about race, racism, and reconciliation.

## 1. WE MUST DECIDE TO LIVE AS GOD MADE US. No matter whether you're red, brown, yellow, black, or white, you're "precious in His sight," as the song goes. It's an affront to God to want to paint your skin any other color than the one God designed for you.

> What steps will you take in the coming months to intentionally embrace
> your ethnicity and the diversity you experience in today's world?

## 2. WE MUST DECIDE TO BASE OUR JUDGMENTS SOLELY ON THE TRUTH, NOT ON ETHNICITY OR ANY OTHER STANDARD. God's Word is the only objective standard that allows us to say, "This is right" or "This is wrong." Our job is not to be popular or culturally acceptable but to live by the biblical truth that all people are of equal worth before God, and all have access to salvation through Jesus Christ.

> What steps will you take to ensure that your actions and decisions
> are based on the truth of the gospel rather than on prejudice?

The truth of God's Word is that, by God's design, all people of all races have sprung up from the same root for the common purpose of bringing glory to our King. God's kingdom agenda demands that we all live in unity with one another.

*Day 5*

# POLITICS AND THE KINGDOM

We've spent this week exploring the implications of God's kingdom agenda for our status as citizens of individual countries and as participants in a broader culture here on earth. Along the way we've waded through some weighty concepts and concerns, including freedom, justice, and racism.

I'll warn you now that things won't get any lighter as we wrap up the week today. That's because it's time to dig into what God's kingdom agenda says about earthly governments and our role as Christians in the political process.

> What emotions do you experience when you think about politics and politicians? Why?

> In what areas of life are you most influenced by local and federal governments?

## POLITICS IN GOD'S WORD

I realize many Christians who are reading this wish they could simply wash their hands of politics and anything connected with governing authorities. Unfortunately, that doesn't make sense on a practical level. More importantly, such a lifestyle doesn't fit with the overarching message of God's Word.

To put it simply, you can't believe the Bible and ignore the political realm. That's because God's Word is thick with politics.

Think about it: large portions of Exodus, Leviticus, and Deuteronomy record the laws and guidelines God gave for the governance of the Israelite community. In the same way, 1 Kings and 2 Kings are two entire books in God's Word that deal exclusively with the rule and reign of government leaders.

The Bible is also filled with accounts of times when God strategically placed people in the political realm in order to accomplish His agenda in the world. He moved Joseph into authority in Egypt, for example (see Gen. 41:38-44), and He elevated Daniel to a position of great influence in Babylon (see Dan. 1:8-21) and later in Persia (see 6:1-3). God placed

Nehemiah in the Persian government so that he could rebuild Jerusalem with government support (see Neh. 1), and He positioned Esther as queen in Persia (see the Book of Esther) in order to save His people from genocide at the hands of an evil political enemy.

Because God is sovereign over His universe, it follows that He's intimately concerned with the political affairs of the nations. That's one reason I like the way David summarized God's involvement in politics:

> *All the ends of the earth will remember and turn to the LORD,*
> *And all the families of the nations will worship before You.*
> *For the kingdom is the LORD's*
> *And He rules over the nations.*
> PSALM 22:27-28

Read the following passages of Scripture and record what they teach about God's involvement in earthly governments.

Psalm 33:6-12

Proverbs 21:1

1 Timothy 2:1-2

What do these verses teach about God's character?

When we read God's Word, we can't escape the reality of God's political activity. That means Christians can't attempt to divide life down the middle, putting God on one side and politics on the other. Instead, we must find a way to connect our lives as members of God's kingdom with our political involvement in government today.

What are legitimate ways we can express our biblical beliefs through political involvement?

Fortunately, we can take our cue from Jesus when it comes to living out that connection.

## GOD'S PEOPLE AND GOVERNMENT

In Mark 12 Jesus was confronted by two religious groups, the Pharisees and the Herodians. These groups normally disliked each other—the Pharisees focused on religious law, while the Herodians were passionate about politics and maintaining good ties with Rome—but they combined forces in a united attack against Jesus:

> *They came and said to Him, "Teacher, we know that You are truthful and defer to no one; for You are not partial to any, but teach the way of God in truth. Is it lawful to pay a poll-tax to Caesar, or not? Shall we pay or shall we not pay?"*
>
> MARK 12:14-15

This was a trick question designed as a trap. If Jesus said not to pay the tax, He could be accused of treason by the Roman authorities. If He said to pay the tax, however, He could be seen as siding with a foreign government that was oppressing His own people. It was supposed to be a no-win scenario.

But verses 15-17 show that Jesus had the number of both the Pharisees and the Herodians:

> *He, knowing their hypocrisy, said to them, "Why are you testing Me? Bring Me a denarius to look at." They brought one. And He said to them, "Whose likeness and inscription is this?" And they said to Him, "Caesar's." And Jesus said to them, "Render to Caesar the things that are Caesar's, and to God the things that are God's." And they were amazed at Him.*
>
> MARK 12:15-17

What are your initial reactions to this passage?

These men thought they had Jesus in a vise, but He sidestepped them by saying, in effect, "Why are you even asking Me this question? You've already submitted yourselves to the authority of the Roman government since you had a denarius to give Me." By using and accepting Roman coins, the Pharisees and Herodians were recognizing Rome's governmental authority. They were benefiting from the government's provision, and Jesus commanded them to give the government what it was due for the services provided.

Jesus affirmed that local and national governments of His time were legitimate institutions and had the right to tax for their services. The same is true for governments today.

What are some examples of services rendered by our government today?

In what ways do we "render to Caesar the things that are Caesar's" (v. 17)?

Jesus' statement included another thought: "Render … to God the things that are God's" (v. 17). This becomes an important point when we remember that everything belongs to God (see Ps. 24:1). He's the Creator of all things. So while Jesus' response legitimized human civil government, it also placed limits on human civil government.

In Romans 13:1 Paul also emphasized the rule of human government under God's authority:

> *Every person is to be in subjection to the governing authorities. For there is*
> *no authority except from God, and those which exist are established by God.*
> ROMANS 13:1

Read Romans 13:1-7. What do these verses teach about our rights
and responsibilities in regard to human governments?

Of course, problems arise when civil governments attempt to overstep the boundaries God has placed around them. In those situations followers of God must live as members of His kingdom first and submit to His kingdom agenda rather than to a government that stands in active rebellion against that agenda. Sometimes righteous agents of God must interpose themselves between an unrighteous government and its innocent victims in order to publicly reflect and defend God's standard. Think of the American civil-rights movement of the 1950s and 1960s, for example.

To be a Christian living in a particular nation doesn't mean isolating yourself from the political or governmental processes of that nation. Quite the contrary. As citizens of both God's kingdom and earthly nations, Christians are called to use every available resource when taking a stand for God's values and God's plan.

Peter wrote that Christians must "fear God, honor the king" (1 Pet. 2:17). If we can live according to those priorities—in that order—we'll do well as citizens of our nation who continually work to advance God's kingdom agenda.

Week 6

# LIVING GOD'S
# KINGDOM AGENDA

# START

**Welcome back to this small-group discussion of Kingdom Agenda.**

The previous week's application challenge asked you to pray for the advancement of God's kingdom agenda in modern society. If you're comfortable, talk about your experiences and any insights you gained through prayer.

Describe what you liked best in the material from week 5. What questions do you have?

How would you summarize the boundaries between the dominion of government and the dominions of individuals, families, and churches?

What ideas or images come to mind when you hear the word *blessing?* Why?

To prepare for the DVD segment, read aloud the following verses.

*How blessed is everyone who fears the LORD,*
*Who walks in His ways.*
*When you shall eat of the fruit of your hands,*
*You will be happy and it will be well with you.*
*Your wife shall be like a fruitful vine*
*Within your house,*
*Your children like olive plants*
*Around your table.*
*Behold, for thus shall the man be blessed*
*Who fears the LORD.*
*The LORD bless you from Zion,*
*And may you see the prosperity of Jerusalem all the days of your life.*
*Indeed, may you see your children's children.*
*Peace be upon Israel!*
PSALM 128

# WATCH

***Complete the viewer guide below as you watch DVD session 6.***

A blessing is the favor of God _____ you that also flows _____ you.

The key to your personal life's success is _____ _____.

Fearing God means to take God _____.

Taking God seriously means you function in light of His _____.

God responds to _____, not merely pronouncements.

When you fear God, it doesn't show up first at church; it shows up first ____ _____.

The reason marriages break down is one or both parties have stopped _____ God.

Reverence brings God's _____ miraculously in your home.

We have a generation of young people today who have no _____ because they have no family.

Children's consciences must be _____, and that job has been given to parents.

The reason God wants you to be a vital, visual part of a local church is so that the family of God benefits from _____ and you benefit from the _____ of God.

God wants to know after you've gone out into the world, what _____ are you going to make?

It ought to be clear that you stand as a representative of the kingdom of God in the public place appropriately, wisely, but _____.

The kingdom agenda starts with you individually, moves to the family, moves to the church, and bursts out into the _____.

# RESPOND

**Use the following questions to discuss the DVD segment with your group.**

What did you appreciate most in Dr. Evans's teaching? Why?

How have you been blessed as a result of your alignment with and participation in God's kingdom agenda?

In what situations do you typically experience the fear of the Lord?

How do you typically react during and after those experiences?

Respond to Dr. Evans's statement: "If you want a better world composed of better states that are made up of better counties composed of better cities inhabited by better neighborhoods illuminated by better churches because they're composed of better families, you gotta start off by becoming a better person. It starts off with your own and my own life under the rule of God."

What are some interesting insights you've gained during this study?

How will you translate those insights into actions during the coming weeks?

**Application.** This is the last time your group will meet to discuss this study, but this shouldn't be the end of your experiences with *Kingdom Agenda*. The material for week 6 is filled with practical assessments and evaluations designed to help you implement what you've learned throughout this study. Please take advantage of them.

**This week's Scripture memory.**

*The fear of the LORD is the beginning of wisdom,*
*And the knowledge of the Holy One is understanding.*
PROVERBS 9:10

**Assignment.** Read week 6 and complete the activities to conclude this study.

## HEARING AND DOING

I believe every verse in the Bible comes from God, and I believe every verse is useful for Christians who are seeking to live God's kingdom agenda each day (see 2 Tim. 3:16). But there are also times when specific passages of Scripture hit us with extraordinary force in specific periods of our lives.

That's been the case on several occasions when I've interacted with the following verses from the Book of James:

> *Prove yourselves doers of the word, and not merely hearers who delude themselves. For if anyone is a hearer of the word and not a doer, he is like a man who looks at his natural face in a mirror; for once he has looked at himself and gone away, he has immediately forgotten what kind of person he was.*
> JAMES 1:22-24

Pow! James's words are like a heat-seeking missile that's targeted directly at our natural inclination to ignore our faults and turn a blind eye to the help we need most. Even now I can't read these verses without experiencing a spiritual gut check. Am I someone who does what the Bible says? Or am I just deluding myself because of what I hear?

I'm highlighting these verses because you and I have heard a lot of information over the course of this study. We've read a lot of material. We've contemplated a lot of ideas. We've seen truth expressed in numerous passages of God's Word. So now we're left with two questions. Will we take action based on what we've heard? Or will we walk away from the mirror of God's kingdom agenda and immediately forget the truth we've seen?

I want you to be a doer of the Word. That's why I've filled our final week together with a variety of activities and assessments specifically designed to help you implement the principles of God's kingdom agenda in your life, your family, your church, and your nation.

As you work through the material this week, remember James's promise to those who do what God has commanded through His Word:

> *One who looks intently at the perfect law, the law of liberty, and abides by it, not having become a forgetful hearer but an effectual doer, this man will be blessed in what he does.*
> JAMES 1:25

*Day 1*
# GOD'S KINGDOM AGENDA
# IN EVERYDAY LIFE

We've reached the final week of our study, and by now I trust you know what I mean when I refer to God's kingdom agenda. It's the visible demonstration of the comprehensive rule of God over every area of life. It's God's blueprint for our hearts, our attitudes, and our actions as individuals, as families, as a church, and as a nation.

Even though we've learned a lot about God's kingdom agenda, you may still be struggling with the critical step of application. In fact, even now you may be pondering questions like these: *Do I really need God's kingdom agenda? Will following God's kingdom agenda actually make a difference in my life? Can it really be worth it to give up control of my actions and attitudes each day?*

I've wrestled with those and other questions numerous times over the years, and I've been forced to wrestle with them again through the process of writing this study. Even so, I believe with every fiber of my being that the answer to each of those questions is yes. And the reason I believe it can be demonstrated with a simple exercise.

> Use the rest of the space on this page to draw several vertical lines freehand. Without using a straight edge of any type, see if you can draw a line that's absolutely straight—no bends or crooked places.

How did you do? Actually, I already know how you did: all of your lines are crooked. Human beings are physically incapable of drawing a freehand straight line. So even if some of your lines look straight, you can be sure there's a bend, a curve, or a wiggle in there somewhere.

However, if you used a ruler or another straight edge, you'd get much closer to an actual straight line. In fact, go ahead and give that a try. Find a ruler or straight edge and draw a line next to the ones you attempted on the previous page. The difference will be obvious.

You see the point: when we attempt to live life on our own, things get crooked. When we try to handle each day through our own wisdom and our own strength—even when we attempt to help others and do good things—we inevitably miss the mark.

But when we submit to God's blueprint for our lives—when we use His kingdom agenda as our ruler for living each day—we have a much better shot at keeping our paths straight:

> *Trust in the LORD with all your heart*
> *And do not lean on your own understanding.*
> *In all your ways acknowledge Him,*
> *And He will make your paths straight.*
> PROVERBS 3:5-6

Why is trust necessary to live according to God's kingdom agenda?

What are some of the crooked areas in your life that need to be straightened out?

How do you currently plan to address those areas?

This week we'll use a number of practical activities and assessments designed to help you bring your life into alignment with God's kingdom agenda. But first let's attack two of the primary obstacles that often keep us on a crooked path.

## OBSTACLES IN THE ROAD

Fear is the first major obstacle that prevents followers of Jesus from fully committing to God's kingdom agenda. Let's be frank. The idea of relinquishing control over our lives is terrifying. That can be true even when we're relinquishing control to God, even though we love Him and know He's good.

The main reason it's frightening to give control of our lives to God is the fact that we don't understand Him. Indeed, we're completely incapable of understanding Him. God is the Creator of the universe. He's the Alpha and Omega. His thoughts are not our thoughts, nor are His ways our ways (see Isa. 55:8-9). Therefore, we fear the idea of submitting to a Being who's completely outside our experience.

Do you experience fear at the thought of submitting your life entirely to the authority of God's kingdom agenda? Explain.

How is fear currently influencing your relationship with God?

So what can we do when fear prevents us from fully committing to God's kingdom agenda? The answer is to change the direction of our fears. Specifically, we must embrace the fear of God rather than allow ourselves to be hindered by the fear of losing control.

That's why the author of Proverbs wrote the following:

> *The fear of the LORD is the beginning of wisdom,*
> *And the knowledge of the Holy One is understanding.*
> PROVERBS 9:10

To fear God simply means to take Him seriously rather than approaching Him casually— and there's a big difference between those two postures.

When have you recently experienced the fear of the Lord?

Most people approach God in a casual way. They believe in Him. They talk about Him. They say grace before meals and go to church on Sundays. And for people who relate to God on that level, the idea of losing control and committing to God's kingdom agenda is certainly terrifying. It represents a total change of lifestyle and direction.

Things are different when we fear the Lord—when we take God seriously and live each day in light of the fact that He sees everything and knows all of our thoughts (see Ps. 139:2). That's because the more we concentrate on the awesomeness of God, the more motivated we become to bend our knee in submission to Him and obey His commands.

> How have you recently encountered the awe-inspiring elements
> of God's character?

Are you ready for the second obstacle that prevents people from fully committing to God's kingdom agenda? It's plain-old selfishness. Many Christians procrastinate when it comes to relinquishing control of their lives simply because they know doing so will rob them of temporary pleasure. It will force them to give up selfish behaviors, or it may require them to exercise greater spiritual discipline in their daily lives.

In other words, many people walk away from God's kingdom agenda because they're having too much fun sinning and don't want to stop.

> Of what sinful patterns or behaviors do you have a hard time letting go?

> What spiritual disciplines or biblical commands have you resisted in recent
> months? Why?

If you find yourself spiritually hindered by selfishness, don't wait until you've figured out your sin problem before turning to God's kingdom agenda. That's backward. You need to submit yourself as fully as possible to God's plan and program as described in this study, then allow Him to transform your sin problem through the work of the Holy Spirit.

## MOVING FORWARD

As we move forward this week, we're going to look at specific, practical ways you can embrace God's kingdom agenda as an individual, as a member of a family, as a member of a church, and as a citizen of this nation. Are you ready?

I'll use Psalm 128 to frame our exploration each day. It's a passage of Scripture that describes the way life was meant to be lived by kingdom people under God's rule:

*How blessed is everyone who fears the LORD,*
*Who walks in His ways.*
*When you shall eat of the fruit of your hands,*
*You will be happy and it will be well with you.*
*Your wife shall be like a fruitful vine*
*Within your house,*
*Your children like olive plants*
*Around your table.*
*Behold, for thus shall the man be blessed*
*Who fears the LORD.*
*The LORD bless you from Zion,*
*And may you see the prosperity of Jerusalem all the days of your life.*
*Indeed, may you see your children's children.*
*Peace be upon Israel!*
PSALM 128

What do you like best about the previous passage? Why?

What do you hope to accomplish this week as you make a practical plan for living under God's kingdom agenda?

*Day 2*
# YOUR LIFE AND GOD'S AGENDA

Today you'll examine your life as an individual in God's kingdom. Look at the first portion of Psalm 128:

> *How blessed is everyone who fears the LORD,*
> *Who walks in His ways.*
> *When you shall eat of the fruit of your hands,*
> *You will be happy and it will be well with you.*
> PSALM 128:1-2

The first thing the psalmist wants you to know is that when your personal life is in line with God's kingdom agenda, blessings will flow from you into all areas of your life—your home, your church, and your community. But it all starts with the choices you make on an individual level.

"How blessed"—how happy—is the person who "fears the LORD" (v. 1). Remember, to fear God is to take Him seriously—to hold Him in awe and reverence. When you fear God, you don't marginalize Him, discount Him, or place Him on the outskirts of your life. Rather, you give Him His rightful place at the center of your existence.

What happens when you fear God? He will take care of your fortune: "You shall eat of the fruit of your hands." He will take care of your feelings: "You will be happy." And He will take care of your future: "It will be well with you" (v. 2).

You may say, "I want to live my life under God's agenda, but how can I know whether I'm doing that?" Good question. The psalmist provided two answers in verse 1: you're aligned under God's kingdom agenda when you fear the Lord and when you walk in His ways.

Over the next few pages you'll evaluate yourself, based on those two criteria. But I want to make sure you understand this isn't a legalistic exercise, nor is it an attempt to judge you or look down on you. Nobody will grade your responses to the following questions and exercises. Rather, this is simply an opportunity for you to reflect on your current actions and attitudes and determine whether any changes are necessary.

We'll start with fearing the Lord.

## FEAR THE LORD

Remember that a main component of fearing God involves recognizing His authority and power in relation to your own. That recognition then causes you to take Him seriously. When you continually recognize that God is the Creator and you're His creation, you're starting down the path of properly fearing Him.

Use the following questions to assess your awareness of these realities.

What steps do you take each day to establish God as your primary priority?

In what situations do you typically feel awe and reverence toward God? Record at least three.

1.

2.

3.

During a typical week how often do you intentionally seek these kinds of encounters with God?

Another component of fearing God involves actually experiencing the emotion of fear when you interact with Him. He is almighty and all-powerful, and it makes sense that you approach Him not only with feelings of reverence and awe but also with trepidation. This is especially true after you've rebelled against Him through active or passive sins.

What emotions do you typically experience when you sin against God?

During a typical week how often do you contemplate the consequences of your sin?

Do your knowledge and awareness of God regularly prevent you from sinning against Him? Explain.

The fear of the Lord is a central component of living as an individual under God's kingdom agenda. So how are you doing?

Based on your responses to the previous questions, how would you rate your current fear of God on a scale of 1 to 10?

| 1 | 2 | 3 | 4 | 5 | 6 | 7 | 8 | 9 | 10 |
|---|---|---|---|---|---|---|---|---|---|
| Little fear of God | | | | | | | | Much fear of God | |

What steps will you take in the coming weeks to take God more seriously and establish Him more firmly as the center of your existence?

## WALK IN HIS WAYS

The second criterion we can use to evaluate our lives as individuals in God's kingdom is determining whether we walk in His ways. In other words, do we actively, intentionally do the things God has commanded us to do? Remember James's words: "Prove yourselves doers of the word, and not merely hearers who delude themselves" (Jas. 1:22).

Use the following questions to assess yourself in this area.

When have you recently felt that God was leading you to take a specific course of action? What happened?

To what degree do you typically seek God's will when you make major decisions? What about minor decisions?

Several passages of Scripture offer key commands for followers of Christ. Let's take another look at three of those passages that apply to you as an individual seeking to live God's kingdom agenda.

*He has told you, O man, what is good;*
*And what does the LORD require of you*
*But to do justice, to love kindness,*
*And to walk humbly with your God?*
MICAH 6:8

How have you recently obeyed God's requirements in this verse?

*He said to him, "You shall love the LORD your God with all your heart, and*
*with all your soul, and with all your mind." This is the great and foremost*
*commandment. The second is like it, "You shall love your neighbor as yourself."*
MATTHEW 22:37-39

How have you demonstrated your love for God this week?

How have you intentionally sought to love your neighbor this month?

*Go therefore and make disciples of all the nations, baptizing them in the name*
*of the Father and the Son and the Holy Spirit, teaching them to observe all that*
*I commanded you; and lo, I am with you always, even to the end of the age.*
MATTHEW 28:19-20

How have you invested your time, talents, and other resources in making
new disciples of Jesus Christ?

Based on your responses to the previous questions, how would you rate
your recent efforts to walk in God's ways?

| 1 | 2 | 3 | 4 | 5 | 6 | 7 | 8 | 9 | 10 |
|---|---|---|---|---|---|---|---|---|---|

I've walked away from God.                              I've walked with God.

*Day 3*
# YOUR FAMILY AND GOD'S AGENDA

The breakdown of the family is the primary cause of many breakdowns we're experiencing in society today. The family touches all areas of life, so it's a crucial battleground both for proponents of God's kingdom and for those who seek to push our culture further and further away from God's values.

What battles for the family are currently being fought in society?

How have these battles affected your family?

Satan understands the importance of the family in a culture. That's why he's always sought to dismantle and destroy the foundations of families, starting with Adam and Eve:

> *The serpent said to the woman, "You surely will not die! For God knows that in the day you eat from it your eyes will be opened, and you will be like God, knowing good and evil." When the woman saw that the tree was good for food, and that it was a delight to the eyes, and that the tree was desirable to make one wise, she took from its fruit and ate; and she gave also to her husband with her, and he ate.*
> GENESIS 3:4-6

Notice that Satan's plan from the very beginning involved enticing families to move away from God's kingdom agenda. When Adam and Eve willingly ate the forbidden fruit, they removed themselves from God's authority and instead operated under their own rule, based on their own authority. The result was chaos both for Adam and Eve as individuals and for their family unit.

What causes chaos in your family today?

Not only did Satan get Adam and Eve to function outside God's prescribed alignment with Him, but he also persuaded them to function outside God's prescribed alignment with each other. Eve became the leader, while Adam became the passive responder. Worse, Adam then proceeded to blame Eve for what was ultimately a lack of leadership on his part. As a result, both shame and conflict entered the family.

Once the family broke down, nature itself began to feel the effect of sin on the world and began to disintegrate as a result of God's curse on the ground. Ultimately, sibling rivalry in the first family led to murder (see Gen. 4:1-15), which then perpetuated itself in dysfunctional relationships among even more families, eventually causing the entire human race to be destroyed except for Noah and his family (see Gen. 6).

Psalm 128:3-4 offers a contrast to these images of chaos and destruction by picturing a family still in line with God's kingdom agenda:

> *Your wife shall be like a fruitful vine*
> *Within your house,*
> *Your children like olive plants*
> *Around your table.*
> *Behold, for thus shall the man be blessed*
> *Who fears the LORD.*
> PSALM 128:3-4

Which blessings do you currently enjoy most as a member of your family? Record at least three.

1.

2.

3.

Families function well when they're in line with God's plan, and ultimately, all areas of society benefit—individuals, churches, communities, and even entire countries. Keep that in mind as you use the following assessments and activities to evaluate your family in light of God's kingdom agenda.

I realize that some people completing this study are single, and others are married without children. If you fall into one of those categories, feel free to focus on the elements of the following pages that are helpful for your own reflection and edification.

# KINGDOM HOUSEHOLDS

As we saw in week 3, the primary mission for every family in the world is to replicate the image of God in history and to participate in His kingdom agenda on earth. Take a moment to evaluate your family in light of that mission.

In what specific ways does your family reflect the values of God's kingdom? Use the following categories to guide your thoughts.

Time:

Money:

Other resources:

How has your family contributed to God's kingdom agenda in your neighborhood or community?

How has your family contributed to God's kingdom agenda as part of your local church?

How do the members of your family contribute to one another's spiritual growth and development?

Based on your responses to the previous questions, how would you rate your family's overall commitment to God's kingdom agenda?

| 1 | 2 | 3 | 4 | 5 | 6 | 7 | 8 | 9 | 10 |
|---|---|---|---|---|---|---|---|---|---|
| Not committed | | | | | | | | Very committed | |

## KINGDOM MARRIAGE

Psalm 128 is directed primarily at men, so that's why the author emphasized the wife's being like a fruitful vine and the husband's being blessed through the fear of the Lord. But we need to remember that vines are fruitful only when they're in an environment that allows them to thrive.

Ultimately, husbands and wives must work together to align themselves under God's kingdom agenda and to fulfill their specific roles in the home.

How have you intentionally demonstrated love and respect for your spouse this week?

To what degree are you able to accept advice and correction from your spouse? Explain.

What boundaries or guidelines have you and your spouse determined in order to align your family with God's kingdom agenda?

As husbands and wives work together, they must also function according to God's desired alignment in the home. Women are aligned under their husbands in terms of ultimate authority, and husbands are aligned under the ultimate authority of Christ.

Do you embrace or resist God's desired alignment for your family?

What steps can you take to further support your spouse's role and responsibilities in your home?

# KINGDOM PARENTING

In speaking of children, the author of Psalm 128 used the imagery of olive plants (see v. 3). In ancient culture olive trees were vital to the success of a family and a society because olive oil was essential for cooking, medicine, lamps, and other uses. Olive trees took about 15 years to mature, however, and required a lot of nurture to eventually produce fruit.

In the same way, parents are called to intentionally nurture their children so that they will one day produce much fruit for God's kingdom.

What steps have you taken to specifically teach your children about God's kingdom agenda?

How often do you intentionally encourage your children?

| 1 | 2 | 3 | 4 | 5 | 6 | 7 | 8 | 9 | 10 |
|---|---|---|---|---|---|---|---|---|---|
| Not often | | | | | | | | | Very often |

How committed are you to disciplining your children in order to raise them in the way they should go (see Prov. 22:6)?

| 1 | 2 | 3 | 4 | 5 | 6 | 7 | 8 | 9 | 10 |
|---|---|---|---|---|---|---|---|---|---|
| Not committed | | | | | | | | Very committed | |

How do you see your children producing fruit for God's kingdom?

Based on your previous responses, what steps will you take this week to further fulfill your kingdom responsibilities as a parent?

Your family plays a vital role in God's kingdom, and you play a vital role in aligning your family under God's kingdom agenda. Take these responsibilities seriously.

*Day 4*
# YOUR CHURCH AND GOD'S AGENDA

I enjoy having microwave popcorn as a treat, especially while I'm watching a football game or a good movie. I also enjoy the process of preparing the popcorn. It's intriguing to watch the complete transformation of hard, coarse seeds into fluffy, delectable treats bursting with a variety of flavors and aromas.

If you don't know the science behind popcorn, this metamorphosis occurs because the microwave heats the water residing in each seed of corn until the water eventually turns to steam. At that point the pressure becomes so great that the shell of the seed can no longer contain the moisture inside, and an explosion occurs. What was once inedible and indigestible becomes edible, digestible, and tasty.

Notice that environment is everything. When the microwave performs as it was intended to perform, the seeds of corn are transformed.

What a microwave is to popcorn, the local church is to a Christian. The church is the environment God uses to transform Christians into what we were created and redeemed to be: mature followers of Christ. Because all true believers possess the Holy Spirit, we already have the internal moisture necessary for that transformation process. We just need the right environment.

Therefore, if transformation isn't happening among Christians, we can conclude that either the seeds aren't in the proper environment, positioning themselves for transformation, or the microwave of the church isn't functioning properly and isn't producing enough spiritual heat for the pressure of the Holy Spirit to "pop" the believer into something new and different.

> What are the major ways you've been transformed from the moment you trusted Christ until now? Record at least three.

1.

2.

3.

I'd like you to contemplate and assess your recent experiences in the local church, but I'm not asking you to evaluate your current church. Although every church has flaws and areas ripe for improvement, that's not what I want you to focus on right now.

Rather, I encourage you to spend some time today assessing your own participation in and contribution to your local church. In other words, are you doing everything you can to place yourself in the right environment for transformation?

## MEETING GOD

In Psalm 128:5 the author wrote:

> *The LORD bless you from Zion,*
> *And may you see the prosperity of Jerusalem all the days of your life.*
> PSALM 128:5

In the Bible Zion was the city of God, Jerusalem, because it's where the temple was located. It was the place where individuals and families came to worship God. Therefore, the closest approximation we have to Zion today is the local church.

Consider these words from the Book of Hebrews:

> *You have come to Mount Zion and to the city of the living God, the*
> *heavenly Jerusalem, and to myriads of angels, to the general assembly*
> *and church of the firstborn who are enrolled in heaven, and to God,*
> *the Judge of all, and to the spirits of the righteous made perfect.*
> HEBREWS 12:22-23

What do you like best about your local church? Why?

Do you view your church as a place where you can meet with and experience God? Explain.

Churches are functioning properly when they help their members experience spiritual transformation, but by no means does everything depend on the church. Followers of Jesus must take responsibility to maximize the environment provided by their churches.

How would you describe your attitudes and emotions about attending church services?

What steps do you take to spiritually prepare yourself before attending church services?

What steps do you take to spiritually prepare your family members before attending church services?

## MEETING AS A BODY

Part of maximizing the environment provided by a local church includes fellowshipping with and learning from the congregation of members in that church. That's because spiritual growth and transformation rarely happen in a vacuum. Instead, we as the body of Christ are called to help and support one another in following God's kingdom agenda.

During a typical month how often do you intentionally and meaningfully connect with other members of your church body?

Who are your three closest friends in your church body? What words would you use to describe your relationship with each friend?

1.

2.

3.

How do you support and encourage the spiritual growth of other people in your church?

Based on your previous responses, how would you rate your level of connection with the staff and other members of your church?

1    2    3    4    5    6    7    8    9    10
I'm isolated.                              I'm well connected.

## CONTRIBUTING TO THE BODY

If you want to align yourself with God's kingdom agenda, your participation in your local church must involve more than receiving. All Christians are responsible to contribute to the life and growth of the body of Christ even as they benefit from church membership.

What gifts, abilities, and resources have you been blessed with? Record at least three that are significant to you.

1.

2.

3.

How do you use those gifts, abilities, and resources to assist your local church in the work of advancing God's kingdom?

How satisfied are you with your current level of financial contribution to your local church?

1    2    3    4    5    6    7    8    9    10
Not satisfied                              Very satisfied

Based on your responses to today's assessments, what steps can you take in the coming weeks to better maximize your experiences in your church?

Many Christians ignore the local church. Only by joining with others in the body of Christ can you discover the life-changing power of Christian fellowship, and only by working with other believers can you make your maximum impact for the kingdom of God.

Kingdom Agenda

*Day 5*
# YOUR NATION AND GOD'S AGENDA

As we come to the final day of this study on God's kingdom agenda, I think it's appropriate that we turn to these hopeful words from Psalm 128:

> *The LORD bless you from Zion,*
> *And may you see the prosperity of Jerusalem all the days of your life.*
> *Indeed, may you see your children's children.*
> *Peace be upon Israel!*
> PSALM 128:5-6

I love the last statement in that psalm. *Shalom* is the Hebrew word translated *peace*. It refers to the well-being experienced in a community when individuals, families, and the church are all rightly aligned with God and with one another. When the different elements of a society function under God's kingdom agenda, you see peace and prosperity in that society. You see a nation that's spiritually healthy.

Unfortunately, that's not the case in our society today. Many people in our culture aren't experiencing peace or prosperity, nor do they have any real hope of ever experiencing it. They won't see their children's children because of the increasing violence, corruption, and corrosion in their communities.

What are some of the biggest problems in today's society? Record three.

1.

2.

3.

We live in a nation that's lost its moral foundation. We're experiencing the chaos that comes from rebelling against God's kingdom agenda. We need to find change and renewal as a society, but most people don't even know where to start looking.

As a follower of Christ, you're aware of these problems because you live in the midst of the mess. But awareness isn't good enough. The real question is, What are you doing about it?

# THE PLACE TO START

Living God's kingdom agenda in your nation starts with you. It starts with your personal walk with God, moves to your relationship with your family, and expands to your involvement in the church. When multiple Christians contribute in those areas, your city, your state, and your nation *will* be influenced. Things *will* change.

That's kingdom impact. But it all starts with you and me aligning ourselves—every area of our lives—under God in order to advance His kingdom agenda.

Having come to the end of this study, how would you evaluate your personal commitment to God's kingdom agenda?

1       2       3       4       5       6       7       8       9       10
Not committed                                                   Fully committed

What steps will you take in the coming weeks to continue aligning yourself with God's kingdom agenda?

What steps will you take in the coming weeks to continue aligning your family with God's kingdom agenda?

What steps will you take in the coming weeks to deepen your participation in and contribution to your local church?

How will you seek support and accountability from other Christians as you pursue the goal of participating in and advancing God's kingdom agenda?

## NEXT STEPS

Bringing about change in your nation starts by aligning yourself with God's kingdom agenda, but there are next steps as well. Specifically, you need to engage your culture and your nation on their own grounds.

We have too many secret-agent Christians today. We have too many covert operatives in God's kingdom who are content with doing their spiritual thing behind the scenes. That's not good enough when the movers and shakers in our culture are actively, openly working against God's kingdom and values.

It's time for you to stand up. It's time for the people in your neighborhood to know what you believe. It's time for your coworkers to know beyond a shadow of a doubt where you stand as a citizen and advocate of God's kingdom. Our nation needs truth; therefore, our nation needs Christians who are willing to stand up and speak the truth, live the truth, and work for the truth in all areas of life.

> How have you actively declared yourself to be a follower of Christ in your neighborhood and community?

> How have you actively declared yourself to be a follower of Christ in your workplace?

> When have you recently had opportunities to take a stand for the truth? What happened?

Because we live in a nation that was established on the principles of freedom and justice, we have opportunities to promote God's values by engaging in the political process. So the next question is, Are you taking advantage of those opportunities?

> How do you participate in the political process?

What opportunities exist for you to combat injustice in your community, in your country, and around the world?

What opportunities exist for you to combat racism and discrimination?

What steps will you take to maximize the opportunities you listed? Record at least three.

1.

2.

3.

How will you lead the members of your family to engage these issues both locally and globally?

How can you work with your local church to promote freedom and justice in your community and around the world?

The kingdom of God isn't an ethereal fairy tale that's located in a far-off land, nor is it a spiritual concept that's limited to our contemplations. No, the kingdom of God is here and now. It's moving forward to complete the purposes God has planned from the beginning of time. The kingdom of God is both our present reality and our future hope.

As subjects of God's kingdom, we live and work under the direct authority of our King. As we've seen throughout this study, we have the responsibility to advance God's kingdom in our world by aligning our personal lives, our families, our churches, and our nation under His authority, functioning according to His blueprint for a productive and meaningful life.

Go therefore and live each day in submission to God's kingdom agenda.

THE URBAN ALTERNATIVE

At The Urban Alternative, the national ministry of Dr. Tony Evans, we seek to restore hope and transform lives to reflect the values of the kingdom of God. Along with our community outreach initiative, leadership training and family and personal growth emphasis, Dr. Evans continues to minister to people from the pulpit to the heart as the relevant expositor with the powerful voice. Lives are touched both locally and abroad through our daily radio broadcast, weekly television ministry and internet access points.

# PRESENTING AN
# ALTERNATIVE TO:

## COMMUNITY OUTREACH

Equipping leaders to engage public schools and communities with mentoring, family support services and a commitment to a brighter tomorrow.

## LEADERSHIP TRAINING

Offering an exclusive opportunity for pastors and their wives to receive discipleship from Drs. Tony and Lois Evans and the TUA staff, along with networking opportunities, resources and encouragement.

## FAMILY AND PERSONAL GROWTH

Strengthening homes and deepening spiritual lives through helpful resources that encourage hope and health for the glory of God.

TONYEVANS.ORG

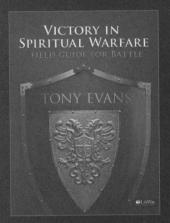
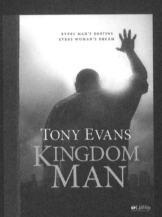
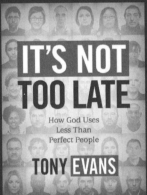